MAN ALIVE

The Making of Men

MARK PETERSON

Artzaintsa Books

Artzaintsa Books

Copyright © 2017 by Mark Peterson
All rights reserved.

PRINTED IN THE UNITED STATES OF AMERICA
21 20 19 18 17   1 2 3

ISBN: 978-0-9898483-6-7

Scripture taken from the HOLY BIBLE, NEW INTERNATIONAL VERSION *. Copyright © 1973, 1978, 1984 by International Bible Society. Used by permission of Zondervan Publishing House. All rights reserved.

Design by Artzaintsa Books

Publisher's Cataloging-in-Publication Data
Peterson, Mark.
Manalive: the making of men/Mark Peterson.
ISBN: 978-0-9898483-6-7 (pbk)
ISBN: 978-0-9898483-5-0 (ebk)
1. Sex—Religious aspects—Christianity. 2. Christian men—Conduct of life. I. Title.
BT708.P48 2017
241'.66 P48
2017949997

CONTENTS

7
PART 1: FIXING THE PROBLEM

29
PART 2: SMALL GROUP — A BIG DEAL

57
PART 3: GO BIG

101
FIVE SMOOTH STONES

A NOTE FROM MARK

This is a book for men. It's short on purpose. Most everything included here I've learned the hard way through the experience of sitting alongside other men in small groups and doing life with them. I have had great mentors and friends (both male and female), as well as many mighty men to sow into over the past twenty years, of which I am grateful. May your life be as relationally full as mine has and may you learn a little more easily than I did. I wrote *ManAlive* in hopes that you do.

In this book, when I refer to "my group" or "our group," I am referring to the ManAlive men's group at my church. I started the group in 2007 with just a few other men. I did it for me. I could impress you with our attendance numbers, but I don't want to count the fighting men. The success of the group continues to rest on the commitment of the men in the room and the love they have for each other.

There are fifteen brief stories scattered throughout the book about men and women whose lives have been changed. No one's name has been changed.

1
FIXING THE PROBLEM

THIS BOOK WAS WRITTEN FOR YOU. IT'S ABOUT SEXUAL PURITY, the foundation that you build the rest of your life on. To get everything you really want in life, you have to get this right first. It's the deepest place you go. It's the core of who you are. It's where you were created, and it mirrors your worship with the living God.

Nearly every man alive struggles at some level sexually. You are not alone. Because this is most men, our primary focus in the group is sexual purity. It's our baseline. If this is not you, translate whatever your struggle area is into its place—whether that's overeating, over-drinking, over-working, the internet, substance abuse, binge watching TV, social media, anger, gambling, shopping, lying, compulsive exercise, cussing, hoarding, video games. . . .This could be a very long list. Know that whatever it is you run to when you're hurting, the pain behind it is the same. Whatever it is, it's killing a part of you that is meant to be alive.

You might get your penis under control, but if what is behind the pain isn't healed, then you'll stop looking at porn and start overeating, etc. It's like a game of whack the mole. You hit one area on the head, but if you haven't addressed the hurt behind it, another problem area will pop up.

The good news is the path to healing is the same too. We're going to give you the hammer to whack the mole. That's how you start getting better. More importantly, you will learn how to position yourself so the hurt can be healed, you find what you really need, learn how to get it, and find what brings you alive. You won't just get free of sexual sin, you'll get free to be a whole, unhindered man who is living an empowered and intentional life. If you have a problem, if there is something that you want to fix, if you want to get better, if you are ready to pursue radical self-improvement, then you have come to the right place.

To get sexually pure you must get naked. You must become known and let others see who you are. Adam and Eve were in the garden naked and not ashamed. They sinned, hid, and covered themselves up, but Jesus died naked on a cross so that we can live naked and not ashamed.

Purity is the prerequisite to great sex. You can have a lot of sex, but you will never have great sex outside of sexual purity, because without it the only thing that can be satisfied is your carnal man. Great sex is hard work and it will cost you. The price is purity. To get there you will need to be honest. Dangerously honest.

The message here is not about controlling your behavior. It's about being sexually free from the inside out, not just sexually sober.[1] I define sexual freedom as the ability to be in a room full of naked Brazilian models and have eyes for only your wife.

If you're single, purity and all that comes with it is preparation for marriage. Prepare well, as you will get what you are. The woman you choose to marry will be different from you in many ways, but she'll be your equal when it comes to your level of personal health. If a man is not sexually pure, marriage does not help get his penis under control; it only makes it worse. It is much easier to work on you when you are still single, so use this time purposefully, because when you're ready, she'll be there. You will find everything you want in a wife when you are everything you know you should be.

If you're in bad shape right now, know that on your journey to holiness it often gets worse before it gets better. What took you ten years to get into isn't going to take two weeks to get out of. It takes time, hard work, discipline, and pain. When you stop whatever stupid thing you were doing, you will feel pain. Pain was there all along, but it was masked by sexual sin, your leading choice of pain management.

If you're screwed up, you are not alone. In my experience (and

---

1. "Sober" in this book is defined as not acting out sexually.

the stats back me), about 65 percent of men in the church and 85 percent out of the church are looking at porn and masturbating weekly, among other more devastating choices of sexual sin.[2] The elephant is in the room and he is so fat you can't see anyone. If you want to get better, your hope lies in the transforming power of Jesus Christ. If you are not a believer now is your chance. Repeat after me and say it out loud.

> *Jesus, forgive me of my sins.*
> *Come into my life and change me from the inside out.*
> *Don't let me go.*
> *Show me what it is to know you.*
> *Help me to follow you wholeheartedly all the days of my life.*

You men who are Christians and didn't pray, know that you are about to experience a second conversion similar to your first. You are about to be saved from hell on earth, isolation. You will fall in love with Jesus all over again through radical honesty and deep relationship. He will unlock the deeper mysteries of who he is and allow you to see life with a totally different perspective. Though having to walk through the consequences of sexual sin would not be my first choice for anyone, a man who has been sexually redeemed is a powerful person. He has no choice but to be. It's a violent battle out. Victory goes to him who is all in, when there is no option but to win. When you dig down deep and you're honest and desperate, the God you have only read about in the Bible will fully come alive to you, his presence felt, his love tangible.

Jesus said if a man lusts after a woman in his heart he has as good as slept with her.[3] For generations of men in Christendom that sentence has been burdensome. It begs the question, "How can I ever live up to that?" The dominant feeling is despair. The

---

2. "Pornography Research," Josh McDowell Ministry, accessed September 20, 2013, https://s3.amazonaws.com/jmm.us.j1ca/Pornography+Research+-+ALL.pdf.
3. Matthew 5:28.

> Joe knew he had to come clean with his wife. He couldn't hold it in any longer and in the parking lot at Costco he broke down and cried as he told her. From the recommendation of a friend at work he started coming to group. He was desperate, and desperate men get better. He is by nature aggressive, so with a few tools he covered ground quickly and got sober right away. Relentlessly, he then began to go after other problem areas in his life wholeheartedly. He was humble and enlisted the help of other men further along in their healing than him. He asked questions, listened, and took action.
>
> At the time, he was ready to lead a group and we had a bunch of men in the room that just were not getting better. So we decided to start an elimination group to either get these guys better or get them out of the room. This was the first group we gave Joe to lead. It was a tough group, but he loved those men consistently and firmly and nearly all of them got better. Two of the men in that group later became leaders and one of them is one of our best bloggers. After that group we nicknamed Joe "The Eliminator."
>
> Since starting group, his career has drastically improved as he has been given a substantial raise every year for the last four years. Additionally he was promoted to director.
>
> He is a faithful servant to the values and purposes we hold dear in the room and has become a natural evangelist enlisting men to join. His presence brings enthusiasm; he is a great speaker and teacher, father, friend, husband, brother, and leader. If you get a chance to spend time with him, take it. It will make you a better man.

good news is that it wasn't meant to be condemning, it was meant to set that standard of freedom. He wants you free from sexual sin from the inside out, not as a whitewashed tomb full of dead men's bones; he is doing the dishes and washing the inside of the cup.[4]

Here is the highlight reel of what you already know. Scripture makes it clear to run from sexual sin and Joseph modeled that.[5] We are to let there not be even a hint of sexual immorality.[6] These are all excellent directives. Yet, he wants all of us right down to

---

4. Matthew 23:26–27.
5. 1 Corinthians 6:18; Genesis 39.
6. Ephesians 5:3.

the core so that there is no lust in the heart. Getting to that place doesn't involve running. Running is a great choice in a place of weakness, but if you want the whole enchilada, to be holy as he is holy, that comes with you taking a stand.[7]

That really hot twenty-year-old you saw downtown today wasn't the devil trying to tempt you. That was the Holy Spirit trying to heal you. Instead of rebuking your thoughts or trying really hard not to look, recognize what is going on. In this battle, you take your thoughts captive by making them submit, taking away their weapons, extracting valuable information, and making them serve you.[8]

Let each tempting situation give you insight into what you really need. The things that attracted you to her will show you. If it was her breasts, you need comfort or nurture. If it was her butt, legs, or belly button then you need acceptance.[9] The point is that whatever is pulling on you puts a magnifying glass on a legitimate need. Your job is to go get your real need met in a healthy way. If you don't find what brings you life, what brings death will find you. If you want to raise the dead, find what brings you life.

Porn is an empty and destructive way of meeting your need for adventure, beauty, discovery, danger, or significance. Once you recognize what you need, transfer that energy to a healthy event. Go on a road trip, cliff diving, hunting, fishing, bungee jumping, skydiving, go to a football game with friends, or climb a mountain. No man will summit a peak over 10,000 feet and beat off. It will never happen. He's fully alive in a dangerous situation filled with the beauty of creation. His God-given need is met.

Learning to recognize the need and getting it met in a healthy way gets you out of the cycle of addiction. If you get triggered by something and call a friend to get some prayer, that's a great move. Keep it up. However, the very fact that you're getting triggered

---

7. 1 Peter 1:15–16.
8. 2 Corinthians 10:5.
9. Russell Willingham, *Breaking Free: Understanding Sexual Addiction & the Healing Power of Jesus*. (Illinois: InterVarsity Press, 1999), 168–173.

shows that you are not taking care of yourself and you have work to do. Get to know you. Learn what your heart needs and go climb that mountain before you see the hot twenty-year-old and you won't give her a second look.

Jesus is the model for purity. Though a man, he was tempted in every way.[10] At the moment when he was weak, tired, hungry, and lonely the devil took him up on the mountain and rolled out the IMAX screen, giving him a fantastic visual, and offered him entire professional cheerleading squads all at once. Jesus said, "No thanks, I'm good. I know who I am, who my Father is, and what I am called to do."[11]

He looked temptation in the eye and stared it down. Like the bronze snake in the desert, God said to look at it and live.[12] The very thing that was killing God's people was what they needed to look at to get better. Ignoring the problem or pretending it's not there is not faith. It's denial. Look at it and live.

HONESTY

> (Jenny) "You ever want to be somebody Forrest?"
> (Forrest) "Aren't I just supposed to be me?"
> *Forrest Gump*[13]

To look at it and live is to be honest. It's easier to live up to the seventh commandment of not committing adultery when we are obeying the ninth and telling the truth. Ephesians 4:25 says, "Put off falsehood and speak truthfully to your neighbor." Most people don't speak the truth because of fear of rejection. If they tell someone who they really are, there is a chance that they can be completely rejected—and that's scary. Most can't handle that, so they play it safe by living in a world where lies of self-protection

---

10. Hebrews 4:15.
11. Matthew 4:8–11; Luke 4:5–8.
12. Numbers 21:4–9.
13. A paraphrased version of the script, *Forrest Gump*, Robert Zemekies, 1994.

are commonplace. People have gotten so far from truth-telling that they start sentences by saying, "to be honest," in order to brace one another for the truth.

Honesty is the doorway to your freedom. Through it you will find everything you have been looking for. If we walk in the light as he is in the light we have true fellowship with each other. Honesty gives us the ability to make true friends that know us and love us for who we really are. When we do that, we receive the full promise of 1 John 1:7, and the blood of Jesus, his son, purifies us from all sin. That's good news.

When we talk about what is really going on inside, it's like flipping on a light switch in the basement; it lets us see what is down there. Opening up gets the junk out and what we need in. We are starved for real relationship. The only way to get the kind of relationships that go down deep and start healing your heart is to let people in and let them know who you really are, what you love, what you would rather do without, what you struggle with, and what is imperfect in your life. We don't want to live two layers deep in the nine-layer bean dip. There is more for us. We want to scrape the bottom of the dish, get down deep and enjoy the whole thing.

We're as sick as the secrets we keep. The question shouldn't be, "Who do I have to tell?" Rather it should be, "Who shouldn't I tell?" A good way to tell if you're getting better is to ask yourself whether you are the same person everywhere you go. If the answer is yes, you're doing it right.

Start practicing honesty by journaling. Don't hide behind religious buzzwords. When you use them you don't have to think about what you're saying. Dig deeper. Be real. Push past the familiar, superficial, churchy expressions and use your own vocabulary to explain yourself. Write in such a way that if your notebook was ever found you would be ruined. David is an excellent example of getting his heart out on paper. Just read though the Psalms to see how it's done. David had problems just like you that he needed God to solve. Honesty in writing and in relationships coupled with abandonment in worship produced solutions in his life. He says in Psalms 32:3, "When I kept silent, my bones wasted away." Lay it all out on the table, men. Confession gives us access to the power of the cross.

Phil is from South Africa. In his twenties he was angered by the sensual billboards advertising strip clubs that hung around Johannesburg. He would go late at night around the city with a knife attached to a long pole and cut them down. His actions caused an uproar from the strip club owners and the local papers nicknamed him the Billboard Bandit. After doing it for an extended period of time with a bounty on his head from strip club owners, he was finally arrested and brought to court.

Phil came to group when he was in his upper thirties. He was soft spoken and had never had a girlfriend. He did great in group, established friendships, was passionate and very committed to the room for the nine months he was here. He did really well at being honest, but he never really was able to get over the wall and establish sobriety.

On his return home he hungered for what he had here and joined one of our online groups. He was able to get sober. More importantly, he started loving himself by finding what he wanted in life and going for it. While in group he met a beautiful godly woman and they started seeing each other. It was satisfying to hear about their time together each week and to see what God was doing in their lives. He was smiling, laughing, and was experiencing joy in their relationship. Everyone in the group knew that she was the one and was sincerely happy for him.

During his share one week he told us that he had broken up with her and mumbled out a bunch of really lame reasons why. We were online but you could actually feel the shock and sadness from the other men in the group. I let him get about halfway through telling us about it before I asked how many in the group thought Phil was running away. It was unanimous. I continued on by saying something along the lines of, "God is obviously on your relationship and she is perfect for you. Sounds to us like you are just scared, but you gotta get over it because the alternative is you growing old, lonely, and weird. Here is what I strongly recommend you do: Get off this call right now, go over to her house, apologize for being a knucklehead, get back together with her, and live the rest of your lives together."

Sitting quiet for a moment, he took the correction like a man with true humility and made the decision to choose to get past his fear of intimacy. They got back together. One year later they were married and are doing fantastic. Since then, he has started

> a business, written a book, had a child, been on National TV, and he and his wife have started both a men's and a women's group in their church, and are growing and thriving together inside and out.
>
> A decade later the Billboard Bandit is back at work in South Africa with his wife, armed with a new vision for themselves, their church, and their country. They are no longer just fighting the symptoms of sexual sin but are passionately going after its roots and by doing so are changing for generations the world they live in.

We're only as honest as we feel safe, so find safe people. Understand that everyone has an intimacy level they can handle. On a scale of one to ten, ten being the most transparent, recognize where others are and meet them there. Outside of your men's group, only be as honest as other people can handle. You might push them a point or two higher on a rare occasion, but if you dial it up too high, you'll lose them. On the flip side, find some dangerously honest people that scare you. They'll be the ones that push you to go deeper. I have a lot of the former and a few of the latter. We need both. Maintain a healthy balance and take it for what it is—a big fat adventure into the unknown of self-discovery.

RELATIONSHIPS

When you're ready to be honest, you're ready for relationship. Sexual sin is a selfish act that hurts others and will isolate you. The more you do it, the further away you get from what you really need. Learn to make and maintain healthy friendships. Become the friend you want to have. Care, ask questions, and really listen to the answers. These are simple acts of selflessness that will pay you back. Do the relational work before you are in crisis so when the trials do come, you're ready with relational change in the bank.

David is the Old Testament model for sexual purity. You know the story. Despite the mess he created with his affair for both his family and his country, he finished well. In fact, he was the only king in Israel's biblical history to give away his throne before his death.

David finished well because he had friends. Samson, who also yielded to sexual temptation, was blinded, mocked, and committed suicide, dying in chains. Though equal in combat prowess and prophetic destiny, the difference between the two was friends. David had them, Samson did not.

The relational structure of David should be aspired to. He had fathers in Jesse, Samuel, and Nathan and peers in Jonathan, Joab, Bathsheba, and Abigail. He also had his mighty men; they protected him, encouraged him, defended him, and told him when he was wrong. They saved his life and helped make David great. When you add mothers to the list of fathers, peers, and mighty men, together these relationships form your own personal phalanx formation. Build that kind of relational structure around yourself and greatness awaits you too.

MAKE FRIENDS

Relationships hurt us, and it's relationships that will heal us. Sexual addiction is a relational and intimacy disorder. Ironically, we have to push into the very thing that scares us the most in order to be healed: relationship. Face the fear, say no to the isolation that wants to kill you, and make friends. Friends = freedom.

When choosing friends, Jesus is the model. The first thing he did right after he came out of an intense time of temptation was figure out who he was going to be in relationship with and what it was going to look like; it's an example of the most powerful use of the prophetic gifting—determining who should be in your life and what it's going to look like. He tapped Peter, Andrew, James, John, and others. He went from temptation to relationship. He spent time with them. They were his closest friends and confidants. He sowed into them and they changed the world. Time = discipleship.

Be intentional about your friendships. The locationships that come with school, work, or sports are not enough. Our heart needs friendships that are pure and not mired in politics, the marketplace, or competition. You have to work at relationship. Call, return calls, hang out, stay up with the current events in your friends' lives. Know what's going on with their work, marriage, and kids. Learn what your friends' dreams are and help them achieve them. Do things they like to do. I like football, but if a friend wants to watch the Stanley Cup, I'm there. I like it because he likes it and I like him. I like steak, but if he is raving about some new Thai place, yeah, let's try it.

Be there for the hard times; do what you can to help. When friends are in crisis, they are usually a little numb and can't think very clearly. Take a pass on saying, "If you need anything, let me know." Few respond to this vague offer for help. Rather, get in your friends' lives and figure out what they do need, then jump in and help them.

Pay attention to who is on your mind. If someone keeps floating through your mind and then starts to hang out in your thoughts, that's the Holy Spirit trying to connect you. Give them a call. You'll be surprised at how many times they'll say, "No way! I was just thinking about you."

The best way to make friends is to find men that are in transition: men who have just moved, have become unemployed, are switching jobs, starting a business, or having a child. The uncertainty and trauma of life's big events open men up to relationship. Most men are really busy and transition in life opens up windows of availability to build a friendship. Find these guys and push in. Encourage them, help them in a tough time, and you'll make a long-term friend.

Friendships change over time. Don't be sad when a friend moves away. Many pull away, but this is a time you can push in. Bless them, help them, and encourage them. When friends move, you have an opportunity to articulate how you feel about them like no other time. To keep these friends, you must keep in touch. I have friends all around the country and a few internationally that I regularly call a few times a year for no other reason than to catch up and maintain the friendship. You can't grow a friendship very well outside of close geography, but you can maintain it. Don't let these friends slip away. You have history together that only time can build. It's work, but it will pay you back. I always tell my buddies that it helps if they move somewhere cool so I can visit and eat their food. God loves me because my friends live in great places like Southern California, Texas, Washington, British Columbia, Colorado, Florida, and Montana. Now I just need a few of them to move to Wyoming, France, Israel, Italy, and the UK.

BE AVAILABLE

To do relationship well you have to be available. Without availability the best you can have is locationships, and that's empty. I made a t-shirt once that said, "My friends answer the phone." The point is that they are available—that's why we're friends.

My favorite word is no. No gives me the ability to say yes. The more I say no to good things, the more I can say yes to great things. I work really hard not to make appointments or live on a set schedule. When I book something, it's usually last-minute, since I want to have an open schedule as long as I can. The most desirable thing

---

When Nick walked into the room he was emotionally shut down, passive, and had only a vague understanding at best of who he was; but, there was hope because he was desperate for help.

As chance would have it he sat in my group and sobered up right away. That first year he was in an intense amount of emotional pain, but he sat in it like a man and felt it. In the middle of his pain he learned to talk.

I gave him as homework Tigers Feeling Wheel, which helps identify and increase our vocabulary on feeling words. As he learned to talk, feelings began to surface that regularly brought tears. Almost every week there were big fat tears slowly running down his face onto his red beard. It was beautiful to see him work through past hurt, rejection, and isolation, and to began to find what his heart really needed. One of the coolest things about this part of his process is that he didn't just break down and weep in group—he kept talking—and as tears rolled down his face he got better fast.

The best part of the story is that Nick broke his long-term pattern of isolation and passivity. Today he has little problem standing up for himself in whatever situation he is in. The constant numbness that used to be the norm has slowly dissolved and he has come alive at work, play, and in his home.

He is an excellent small group leader and now with great zeal runs our online groups as well. He is big but gentle, a truth-teller yet encouraging, compassionate but firm. He's a man you want on your team, a man of prayer, and best of all his marriage is solid. He and his wife are in love, best friends, and growing.

about being self-employed is the freedom to schedule your own life. You will work harder, but it's on your own terms. Availability = relationship.

ACCOUNTABILITY DOESN'T WORK

I don't like the word accountability. Someone mouthed that word at Promise Keepers twenty years ago and it's been preached like it's the gospel ever since. Accountability is not in the Bible, and it doesn't work. I hear terms and phrases like "accountability group" or "I need you to keep me accountable" all the time. Absolutely not. I won't do it, and I categorically reject the word in that sense. Accountability wants me to be a policeman, and I refuse.

Men hide behind accountability all the time. It shifts the weight of responsibility off the man who should carry it, and onto the man who shouldn't. What men want, what men need, is relationship—not accountability.

FORGIVENESS FREES YOU

Unforgiveness keeps you in your own personal prison that will, over time, turn into bitterness. If you're going to have healthy relationships that get you better, then you're going to have to learn to forgive. People will let you down and we have to be able to let it go. Life is a big experiment in failure. Being right doesn't help you in relationship. Being wrong and owning it does. If you have wronged someone, go and make it right. Use the words, "I'm really sorry I did that, will you forgive me?" If your actions caused someone financial loss, make amends with your checkbook as well as your words. When we work through something hard that affected a relationship and come out good on the other side, it only deepens the friendship.

When we pray for those who have hurt us we're not giving them a pass. We're asking God to do a transformational work in their lives. These things hurt in all the right ways, just as God's transforming work in your own life is painful to get you where you need to be. We can't chase everybody down and fix every relationship because we only have control of our side of things. Forgiveness doesn't always mean reconciliation, but it does mean that I am good on my side. Forgiveness is a supernatural event that takes place on the inside and is preceded by our choice to let go. Forgiveness frees us to love and to be loved. Forgiveness = friendship.

FIND THE RIGHT SOURCE

God uses relationships to heal us, but even the best relationships don't outweigh our relational need for God. Sometimes it's easier to make a call than to pray. Jesus is your source. He is our healer, our provider, our father. When we try to find what we need from men that only he can provide, we come up empty. Learn to distinguish what type of relationship you need at different times in your life—that of your friends, or intimacy with your God.

I recently went through a very dark spiritual time. If I had to rate it (I like to rate everything) it would have been the second hardest time spiritually for me in the last twenty years. I went to a lot of counseling, sometimes twice a week. I was mad, sad, and hurting. A large majority of my closest friends didn't even know what I was going through. They knew I was hurting, but I didn't tell most of them all the details and for the ones I did tell, I kept it brief. I knew they couldn't help me and I didn't want to pull them down or cash in any of my relational change. What I needed and what I got, I could only get from heaven.

So it is with all our relationships. Not only do we have to know what we need; we have to discern what others need as we're interacting with them so we can point them to the source if they aren't meant to get what they need from us. If we don't make the right call, trying to help them can feel like getting pulled under by a drowning man, and we end up wasting time and energy, and losing relational equity, not gaining it. No amount of personal relationship can help some people at certain times in life, it has to come from God. He has what we need.

USE THE TOOLS

Being honest and building relationships are the two non-negotiable tools that you must use to get sexually pure and get better in any of the areas you are struggling. The following list will also help you, but know that tools only buy you time. Each one has its place. Use

PART ONE FIXING THE PROBLEM

Amanda's Story: I knew of my husband's porn problem before we got married, but not before I fell in love with him. I thought he just needed a good wife who would nurture and love him right out of his problem. I thought, "We'll get married, I'll stay fit and sexy and attentive to his sexual desires and bam, the problem will be solved." How wrong I was, and how little I understood about the consuming and destructive nature of porn during those early years.

For fifteen years our support system was nonexistent. We learned not to share our struggles because the few times we had, it seemed to only add to the isolation and didn't give us any real answers for freedom. ManAlive changed everything for us. It was like a flashlight to the soul. Before, my husband didn't have hope that life could be different. He had tried other purity groups, and even leaders within the church would say addiction to porn was just something he'd have to live with for the rest of his life. In ManAlive he learned the truth that he could be free from porn. He chose to be brave and look at his pain, and by learning new coping and relational skills, he began to change and heal from the inside out.

Now he knows who he is, what brings him life, what brings him pain, and what to do with that pain in a healthy way. He is brave. He is manly. He's confident. He plays. He interacts with other men. He is hopeful, adventurous, and more balanced. There are no more real lows, no more depression, no more dark isolation causing him to retreat into fantasy or into his head. He is more present. He is more mentally and emotionally stable and available to me and our children. He is a good provider, a hard worker, an excellent communicator, and I trust him completely. My heart is at peace because of that trust and I have been able to love more fully. Sex is no longer complicated—it's just amazing (the way it was always intended to be)!

For over twenty years my husband has wanted to own his own business, and had started and failed many times. But now with a clearer brain, a stronger self-esteem, and solid character he successfully owns his own business. He has learned about determination to never give up. On a practical financial level our children can attend private schools, get braces for their teeth, and discover the world through travel—all because their father has done the work to heal his heart, spirit, and mind. As the head of the family heals and finds freedom, so does the rest of the family. ManAlive, WomanAlive, ChildrenAlive, FamilyAlive, CommunityAlive, CityAlive, CountryAlive. It begins at home. One man's freedom has huge potential to shape and impact his family and the rest of the world.

them; they keep you from doing something stupid. In the end we need Jesus to heal us. But to free us from the desire for dumb while we wait for him to finish what he's started, we need the tools. They position us for an encounter with the living God, and that's where we are healed. These are the basic blocking and tackling drills that win games. I like trick plays as much as anyone, but they only work when the fundamentals of the game are done right. Train yourself and use them well.

Tools that Build the House of Holiness

1. GET IN A GROUP. This is covered in the next section of the book in detail, and I spend a fourth of the book on the dynamics of small group because it's important, very important. This is a team sport, not an individual event. We need each other. If you do not have access to a group near you, I strongly recommend getting in one of our online groups before you start your own. For more information go to imanalive.com.

2. WORSHIP. Worship is warfare. It is anything that brings intimacy with God. Worshipers get well because worship fills your heart with what you were created to hold.

3. CALL SOMEONE. When you call when you're in trouble, you win. The call gets you in the light and breaks that isolation; it's a reminder that you are not alone. It's an act of humility that says, "I need help. Can you pray for me?"

4. GET RID OF ANYTHING DRAGGING YOU DOWN. Internet, smart phone, negative relationships, video games, alcohol, TV, social media, movies, even geographical areas. You may even need to switch jobs. When we purge the unhealthy and unnecessary from our lives, it makes room for the good that God wants to do. Nothing on the list needs to be avoided permanently, only for a time as you establish purity or work your problem area.

5. EAT RIGHT. Fuel your body with real food made from scratch. Get away from as many processed foods as you can. Go heavy on the fruits and vegetables, and eat organic as often as you can. When you eat good, you feel good, and you do good.

6. REST. Failures happen when we are tired. Patton said, "Fatigue makes cowards of us all." I take a nap almost every day. I get some grief for it from people, but it's a game changer for me. Take comfort that great men often nap. Stonewall Jackson and Napoleon would take naps during pitched battles. Churchill napped an hour a day even during the bombings of London. Naps give you the best of both worlds, you can stay up late and get up early, and as long as you take a nap, you're good.

7. DISCIPLINES. There's a great book on this that any man who wants to get his penis under control should read called *Celebration of Discipline* by Richard Foster. It covers the disciplines of prayer, meditation, study, fasting, simplicity, solitude, and service.

8. ACTIVITY. Our bodies need to move. If you're not into working out at a gym, choose to do chores, sports, swimming, physical labor, or the hiking that goes with hunting or fishing. It feels good to get the blood pumping. It gets our heads clear so we can make good decisions.

9. WORK. Men need to work; it's who we are. It's amazing what a few months of hard manual labor will do for the soul. When you get paid, pay your bills on time and stay out of debt. Live simply: less is more, stress is less. Work hard, play hard, rest easy.

10. COUNSELING. Sometimes we need a pro to help us look in places we wouldn't have gotten to on our own. Find good counselors by referral. Good counseling deals

It took Aaron almost two years of coming to group to sober up. Once at a party I asked his wife, "What drew you to him?" She said, "His intellect." I had never asked that question of anyone before and it told me a lot. It's true. Aaron is smart, really smart, but he was stuck in his head and was also struggling with his faith for the first time.

After sitting in the room and hearing our speakers say over and over that honesty, vulnerability, and aggressiveness gets you better, it started to sink in to the point that he was able to get over his brain and go for it. He started by going home and sharing his past hurt with his wife and he was able to cry in front of her for the first time. He told the story the next week in front of the whole room and started a chain reaction of men going home and doing the same thing with their wives. For a month straight fantastic standing-ovation testimonies kept being shared because of what Aaron had started.

He did that same thing with God. Aaron trusted him with what he couldn't explain or understand and was able to be fully honest about his feelings of being abandoned by God. He also went to counseling with Andy Flaherty (the king of vulnerability from the pulpit) and got his balls crushed regularly. For a time it really helped him to limit things that were bringing him down so he could stay sober. He also pieced together that his struggle with porn and masturbation were a cover for his fear of vulnerability. So he did what men do, he ran toward the fear and went to the extreme in personally honesty.

All this was a massive convergence for him as his wife started a successful online business and along with him getting a big raise at work they were able to buy their first home. Though a bit nervous he started leading a small group and did great, and his first time speaking in the room he crushed it. It was one of the best talks of the year for sure. We couldn't podcast it because it had way too many personal details we weren't comfortable with everybody hearing and we had to edit so much of it that there was hardly anything left. The effect of his speaking on the room was nothing less than infectious enthusiasm that led us toward greater collective vulnerability.

His marriage is better than ever and his wife is a passionate evangelist for the group. He went from being sort of in, to all in. The passivity is dead. Today he is one the most committed men in the room, one of our best speakers, and he rose to such of level of respect in the room that he ran the group for me this past summer while I was away. When you get the chance listen to a few of his podcasts, you'll like them.

with the origin of the problem and brings healing to that place. It digs into the past and gets you current with today.

There are not just ten "tools to handle your tool," there are hundreds, but these are some of the main tools that will be a huge help in getting sexually sober and get a handle on whatever life-sucking habit you're using for pain management. The most important thing they do for you is position you for a touch from the Lord that brings deep healing so that you are not just sexually sober but inwardly free.

Tools hold you down and let Jesus heal you. An encounter from God in our lives keeps us from being the guy who brings a knife to a gun fight; it levels the playing field. No matter how good we get at being honest, building relationships, or using the tools, it's God's presence that transforms lives from the inside out. Time and again, God has met me when I'm at the end of myself with waves of supernaturally felt love, acceptance, and divine circumstances. We have what we need to be holy as he is holy because he has made a home inside of us.

There are many more tools, some of which will be covered in the next section about small groups. Many others you will learn for yourself the hard way and by watching the lives of other men in the group you join. In your small group you'll have a front row seat at a life lecture on what works and what doesn't. Time and experience will be your favorite professor.

LITTLE BITS OF BETTER

We are going after better. A better man—a better husband, a better father, a better friend, better with money, a better listener, kinder, and more encouraging. Better is the goal. Improvement, a little at a time. The moment you start to get better sexually and sober up, a whole new world of better opens up. You begin to see how messed up the rest of your life is and you want to make it better, a lot better.

Now it would be great to just have this huge turnaround . . . like, bam! "Hey Mom, I'm all better now." But it doesn't work that way. Most of the time you say to yourself, "I want that," and you go for it. You do the work, you think, you ask for help. Mostly you just work really hard at it and when it gets frustrating because you're not getting much better, or you don't think you are, that's about the time you have a moment when the work pays off. The stars align, and you get a little bam! Maybe not the big one you were looking for, not the lottery ticket, but something good happens and the pieces fall together and you realize that you're better. Welcome to life. You're growing up, and this is how it works.

At ManAlive we applaud better, even a little bit, something, anything. Better is what we are going after because we know that a lot of little bits of better over time make a better and more whole man.

2

SMALL GROUP A BIG DEAL

I CAN'T SAY ENOUGH, GENTLEMEN, ABOUT HOW IMPORTANT A SMALL group is. If you had to choose one thing to do to get better, choose to be in a small group. If there's not already a small group that you can join near you then you'll have to start one because you need it for you. Not only that, the men at your church need you to start a group. They've been waiting for you to do it. The need is huge and the opportunity is great, the reward is even greater.

If you have already been in ManAlive in Redding, or in another one of our groups around the globe then you are in great shape to start one. You've seen it modeled, know how it's done, tasted the atmosphere, and experienced the life-changing dynamics. You have seen the fruit. Now you can recreate it, but more than that you want to recreate it—you want to help other men the way you have been helped.

If you have not been in a group prior, I strongly suggest that before you start one in your church you first join one of our online groups. Get the info and sign up at imanalive.com. Once you've been in one of our online groups for at least six months, you'll know what to do, how to do it, and have the additional bonus of a built-in mentor to call when you need help.

Starting this group is a noble task worthy of your greatest effort. It's a smart move that will pay you back—not just you, but your family, church, and community as well. And not just today or next month, but for the years and decades to come through the lives of men you sow into.

In small group, we work on the whole man, not just his penis. Guys come to group for a carburetor adjustment and end up getting a full engine rebuild. The cool part about a group where the starting point is what a man does with his penis, is that it addresses the very most important thing in a man's life. There is no deeper place you can go than your sexuality, so the intimacy in the group is unparalleled.

Helping men get better is a high call that you will love. They need help, we have the answers, and the best part is that you'll get better too. You were created to lead and this group will draw out your greatness. Some men fail, but most grow like summer corn.

You won't be able to fake it; the others in your group will smell that a mile away. You will have to gut yourself regularly. If you don't, you will lead in title only, because the most vulnerable man in the room is the most powerful man in the room. Men follow courage, not titles. Be courageous.

This section is a combat leader's field guide for how to lead a small group. It will help you get men sexually pure and free, not just sober. Do the group for you. If it's not good for you, it's not good for anyone. It is impossible to love your neighbor as yourself if you don't love you.[1]

It's your assignment to get these men clean. You can do the one-step, the twelve-step, or the Texas Two-Step; it doesn't matter to me how you go about it, just that you get it done. You will be surprised by your ingenuity, and in time you will add to this Wikipedia of mastery in leading men. Your true long-term success will be determined not in how many men you lead in getting better, but how many group leaders you create along the way.

If you think this is an addiction support group and an accountability ministry, you have it all wrong. I have a strong dislike for all three of those words, and if you want to get men free and not just sober, you will too. What works and what we do in a small group

---

1. Leviticus 19:18; Mark 12:31.

PART TWO **SMALL GROUP**

is completely relationship based. Relationships hurt you, and the irony is that it's relationships that will heal you. Men are lonely because they have been hurt and relationships are dangerous and scary. A man will speed climb the Eiger and risk his life, but die

> Kenny left group after being angry at me that he had to pay to get in a small group. He came back a month later, paid to get in, and as chance would have it, he landed in my small group. I told him, "I don't go easy on anyone. You should wait until next week and get another group leader."
>
> He insisted on being in my group. Within minutes of his first share, I recognized that he had a lying problem. The homework I gave him that week was to find four people that he had lied to, confess, and ask for forgiveness. He went pale. I thought I would never see him again and was surprised the following week when he came back. During his share he started crying as he talked about how his homework went. He said, "I told my boss that I had called in sick when I wasn't sick." His boss said, "It makes me trust you that you told me that," and immediately his boss began to open up to him like never before.
>
> He had lied his whole life, so I kept giving him that same homework every week and every week he came back crying with a new story about what had happened.
>
> One week he could barely speak he was so emotional. He is retirement age and has to take pill to keep an erection, but was weeping uncontrollably as he told us that he just had the best sex of his life with his wife, Viagra free. He said that for the first time in his life, he felt like there was nothing in-between them. It was beautiful and more intimate than they had ever experienced.
>
> He's been in group two years and hasn't stopped crying. He's about to make leader, and he's up to speak this summer at group. He attends a small church in town and has had many people there openly crying as his testimony has affected everyone in the congregation. He's gone from not having enough to sharing what he has. His wife just threw him a two-year sobriety party where members of his family, once estranged, all came to celebrate. He is a changed man, and is affecting change in everyone around him. His countenance glows and he's always smiling the smile of gratitude. Want one of the best hugs of your life? Go find Kenny, he'll give it to you.

lonely. To get better you have to do danger. To get others better you must model it.

MY JOB (AND YOUR JOB) IS NOT DONE UNTIL:
You are having the best sex of your life.
You have an enviable marriage.
You have friendships that others want.

STARTING YOUR GROUP

First, get the blessing of your pastor. Keep it low-key. Say something along the lines of, "Hey pastor Bob, I want to start a men's group in our church with the initial focus of going after sexual purity. I am just going to start with a few men and see how it goes. Will you bless me?" Get prayed up and go for it. The response you get will be positive because your pastor has been praying for you to step forward and do it. The church has a problem, and the men's group you are about to start is the solution.

Next, find some men (at least two and no more than six—that's seven including you). It won't be too hard because the vast majority of the men in your church are struggling sexually. Use your prophetic gifting to identify who to invite. Be purposeful about it, as each one of those men will be your future leaders (See Part 3).

Don't advertise or promote the group. A changed life is your promotion. Good restaurants don't need an advertising campaign. You want to stay undercover for as long as you can. Let the fruit of changed lives speak for itself.

In your group, you'll talk about what went on during the week and any major events that might have stirred up some issues. You'll talk about your successes, your failures, what you're scared of, what hurts, what you want to do, what you're not doing, and all the whys behind this stuff. You're letting men get to know you and giving them a window into your life, and they're doing the same. As the men in your group communicate all this, you can see where they are and what they need. The group leader models how to do this, and asks questions to draw the men out and get them talking.

Break the paradigm of "another program" (because this isn't a program) and meet together outside of the group. Eat together; help each other outside of the room. Be men together. Have fun.

LEAD LIKE YOU

Your group should look like you and not like anyone else. Copy someone only long enough to find who you are, then run with it. Your men need you a lot more than they need a formula or a program. I have yet to see a man be a great group leader his first year. If you are about to start leading, I hope you will be the first. In your second year you're pretty good. Your third year you're great, and on your fourth year you can teach it. The point? It takes time.

You all may not have been mentored perfectly, if you were, there would be no need to read this book. The information here will help a bit, but the short of it is that you just need to crawl down in the trenches and get a shot at it, make mistakes, and see what works and what doesn't. The biggest thing is commitment. The most committed leaders are the best leaders. Be there every week, listen, love, pray, and encourage, and your men will transform over time right before your eyes. It's pretty cool.

The South had great generals; it liked them religious and a bit mad. After you have built trust, be a little crazy; your men will love you for it. Patton rightly said, "I have never had a great commander who is not a prima donna."

ONE RULE

We only have one rule in small group and that is confidentiality. Nothing leaves the room. If your pastor asks about someone specifically, respond by saying, "Sorry, I am bound by the confidentiality of the group." This makes it safe for a man to say what he needs to say to get better.[2]

---

2. Confidentiality doesn't cover situations when the law is being broken. Your pastoral oversight should be notified in cases that are in question.

You're going to hear some things that will be hard to listen to in your small group. Avoid judging other men by understanding and focusing on what is going on with them on the inside, not on the act itself. Religion wants to judge outward actions. There are reasons why men in your group do what they do. Find the reasons and let go of whatever dumb thing they did and give them grace. God forgives us through the act of confession. Many men have trouble receiving forgiveness, so let your response to their screwups be a reaction that frees them from shame and guilt. It's easier not to be mad at or judge a man when you understand his past. So get some history and keep focused on the inside of the man. When you see the guys in your group like God sees them, you'll have compassion coupled with vision for them. Men get better fast in that type of environment.

Not being judged is a gift that you want too. Feeling judgment from others when we're risking being honest is a real bummer, but we have to care more about getting better than we care about what other people think of us.

THESE ARE NOT RULES BUT STRONG SUGGESTIONS:
No cross-talking or interrupting.
Pray vertically, not horizontally.[3]
No church words.
Show up every week unless you are out of town or hospitalized.

GROUP SIZE

Seven men is max group size—a leader and six guys works best. If you have eight men in a group and everybody shows up, split the group in half (with the healthiest guy in the group leading for the night) so each man can have more time to talk. The leader needs to be there a minimum of five out of six weeks—that's just minimum attendance. If you do have to miss a group, it's not always a

---

3. Vertical prayers are prayers to God. Horizontal prayers are prayed to be heard by others.

Ken, a leader on Monday night, was speaking at our Friday night service at church and for the first time publicly telling his story about his past same-sex attraction. It was powerful.

Rodger, whom I had known fifteen years prior as an elder in our church, was visiting from 300 miles away that night. After the service he came up to me and with tears in his eyes said, "Ken's story is my story." As he said the words he just broke down and started weeping. I had known him for a long time as a gregarious, funny, tender-hearted leader and teacher, but had no clue that he had ever struggled at any level with homosexuality.

We met the next day and he asked what I thought he should do. I said, "Why don't you just move here and come to group?" So he went home, left his job, sold his house, and was here in months. The move was life changing.

In group, he found a place where he was welcomed, loved, and honored as a man and that embrace was deeply healing for him. With some time in the room, he realized that the majority of the things he struggled with were common to all men, not just unique to those struggling with homosexuality. Once over that barrier that had isolated him, he was off and running. He kept getting better and built great friendships that were healing both to him and the men and women he was in relationship with.

He sobered up immediately and within the year was leading a group. He courageously and consistently puts himself out there with an honest inventory of where he's at, and this has been a huge part of his ongoing path to getting better.

Though still in process like the rest of us he has become a leader of leaders, super encouraging, and a fantastic speaker. There is hardly a group leader in the room that doesn't pull on him with questions, lean on him for relationship, and count him as a friend.

Today he counsels men professionally both here and online and he is great at it. If you need help beyond small group, he is your man. With a deep love for the church he is focused on playing his role to help the church see and think about sexuality correctly. He has a lot of hope for what we can be and is courageously taking radical personal action to make that vision happen. Look for him on our podcasts and through the resource tab on our website, imanalive.com. You will be happy you did.

negative as thing as it gives another guy in the group a chance to lead without you.

Leaders are strongly encouraged to take at least six weeks off during the summer or during a time of the year that works better for them. This gives one of the other men in the group a chance to lead, and allows the leader to unplug, refocus, and come back ready to go.

CIRCLE OF LIFE

Sit in a circle, not an oval, or worse, at a rectangular table with you at the head. The circle says, "We are in this together. There is nothing between us, and I am on equal ground with you." If a guy is making eye contact and talking only to me because I'm the leader, I say something like, "I'm not the only guy in the group. They are going to help you as much as I am, so talk to everyone in the group when you speak." Just keep putting back on the group anything they want to put on you. Remember that you're always trying to work yourself out of a job, so help train your men to pull on each other, and not just you.

TREAT EVERY MAN THE SAME

On average, we have one guy in each small group who is struggling with homosexuality. I try to treat every man the same, and resist the urge to treat them specially. Love them, hug them, treat them like a man. What's really cool is that they get in a group with six other guys and over time everyone in the group comes to understand that it's the same pain, it's just manifested differently. It's healing for everyone in the group. It's deeply satisfying to watch the process of men finding acceptance, love, and understanding. Over time many of these guys begin to date, get married, have kids, and build a family. It's a beautiful thing to be a part of.

I have two men in my small group this year that showed up struggling with same-sex attraction. I asked Rodger, a long-term friend of mine and also a leader in the room who has worked through same-sex attraction, what kind of homework should I give these men that might be different from from what I normally give. He said, "Have them do non-spiritual things outdoors with other men." I've been giving them that homework every week along with other homework and it has worked wonders. Both men are doing great. Trevor, since joining group and sobering up right away, started dating his first girlfriend, and is doing great—so good in fact that when I missed a group last week I left him in charge.

Though I am no expert, I have friends who are: Rodger Gaskin and Ken Williams. Both leaders and speakers at ManAlive, they (along with Elizabeth Woning, who is really incredible too) started Equipped To Love, which serves people impacted by homosexuality. I absolutely love what they are doing and regularly sit in on their talks. It's fantastic, so good that I often cry. You can connect with them at equippedtolove.com or through the counseling tab at imanalive.com. Even better, have them come to your church and speak. Fly them out first class, put them up nice, feed them well, and pay them generously. They're awesome, you'll be glad you did. These three are on the forefront of articulating the church's position and correct response to homosexuality and culture. More importantly they are showing the way out to many and giving hope to the hopeless. They're ambassadors of healing.

FIRMNESS IS KINDNESS

It has to be okay with you if guys leave. Either drive them into the group or out of it. Allow no middle ground. You don't want them to leave, but until you bring them to that place of decision, they can't get better. You are their friend when you tell them the truth, no matter how hard it hits them. That's kindness. You have to be okay if you never see them again.

When interacting with your men, always remember that firmness is kindness. If you love these guys, you will tell them the truth and they will thank you for it later. You cannot softly love men to better (new leaders try this all the time and fail). I give guys in my group about six weeks at the most of nice. I'll let a few things slide at first, but not for long. That month and a half of grace gives them some time to settle in, build trust, and for us to get some relational history. At that point, if a guy is stuck, I start to turn up the heat with tough questions that get him out of no-man's-land.

Remember that you're doing this group for you, so train the men in the group how to listen, how to talk, how to touch, how to feel, how to act, and how to pray so that it's a group that you want to be in, a group you want to share your deepest stuff in. If you have a lousy group, it's no ones fault but yours. If you don't like it, change it.

I just watched about five seasons of *Biggest Loser* with my family. There are two trainers, Bob and Jillian. Jillian is tough yet compassionate with her clients. She gets in their heads. They cry, they get mad at her, but she gets results and they love her in the end. Bob is great. Everybody loves Bob and wants to have him as a trainer. However after six seasons against Jillian, only one of Bob's people had won the title. It has been enjoyable to watch Bob get tougher over time. He actually started yelling at people. I love it. He stopped putting up with their crap. He stopped rescuing and he started to win.

TIME

Managing your group time is a huge factor. If you respect it, the men will respect you; plus you'll get a lot more done by limiting the time, not just letting it run you. If I have a full group I give each man five minutes to talk. I use the stopwatch on my phone as the timer and lay it on the floor in the center of the circle so everyone can see it. When he is getting close to the end of his time, I reach down and pick it up to signal that his time is almost over. If one of my guys is having an unusually deep share or crying when they reach the time limit I will say something like, "You can have one of my minutes." This doesn't cut him off, but it does put pressure on him to wrap it up because he is taking from the group leader's time and that is valuable.

A full group of seven guys each with a five minute share takes thirty-five minutes. If I don't have a full group I will extend the share time a few minutes per man to the point that we hit around the thirty-minute mark. That time frame works great, so try to stay in that time zone and you'll be golden.

Limiting each man's share time does a bunch of stuff for you:
- It keeps the diarrhea mouths from running on and on, which ruins small groups around the globe (a universal time limit, described above, would solve the problem).
- It draws out the men who don't know how to talk. At first they will only say a few things with little meaning because they have never been listened to before and don't know what to do with it. Let them sit in the quiet. Honor them with the group's time. Ask them a question to keep them going. I have seen many a man's man cry over this as they try to speak because someone finally cared enough to listen and to value them. It's glorious.
- It helps men learn to articulate themselves quickly and precisely. This is the most important benefit of watching the clock; it's huge because guys need to learn this to get better and stay better.

The guys in your group are learning to get a lot said in a short amount of time. When this is learned, it goes so much better for them because no one outside of the group is going to let them ramble on for five minutes unless it's a paid shrink. On the outside you will get thirty seconds, not five minutes, and this is practice.

A good homework assignment is to get men to practice what they are going to talk about in the mirror at home before they show up so it flows. This will pay them back down the road in every part of life.

Leave time to pray and prophesy over each other at the end of each group. (If you are an evangelical, all that means is encouragement and to give them hope for the future.) If a man can see his future he can get through his crap. Find God's heart for your men and you will fall in love with them. I can't tell you how many times I have started a new group and thought, "Man, these guys are jacked up. I don't like anyone in this group at all," only to later on love each one deeply.

Prayer time at the end of group can eat up a lot of time too, so manage it. When I start a group I usually pray a lot to model how it's done: short, precise, and to the point. I am praying over what I heard them talk about, inviting God into the situation. I mix prayer with prophecy and encouragement, being very clear on how God sees them and letting them know we believe in them.

I don't like the prayer time to run on too long, so I limit prayer to two men praying for each man so it just keeps moving along. I usually have the guys stand (since we've been sitting for a while now) and have the man we're praying for in the middle. As a group we put our hands on his shoulders as we pray for him. This is a great time to train your men how to pray, for them to simply learn that it's just a conversation with God. Don't allow any hyper-religious words, or horizontal fix it prayers. Just normal, God-connecting, humble but confident speech is what we're looking for.

Until your men are trained, you'll often have one guy who is a ball hog and wants to pray for everyone and rambles on using a bunch of church words for several minutes. Stop this before it happens by teaching on it before you pray. Say something like, "Hey men, we have the no church words rule in group, that also transfers to the prayer time. Let's have two men pray for each man, one minute or less each so we can get home to our families. And please don't try and fix anyone with your prayers. It's up to them to do the work. We're here to pray for them and when they do their part, God will do his."

SHARE ORDER

Who shares first each week in group is important. If the group is just starting, you should always share first to model how it's done.

Go crazy deep, give them information they could hurt you with, show them with your share how you got better, why you keep getting better.

One thing I like to do before we start to share each week is to ask for a show of hands who made it sexually this week. If someone had a failure, I will start with the guy next to them and go around the circle the opposite direction so the guy who had the failure goes last. This does a couple things. First, there is a bit of corporate recognition that happens when the guys get acknowledged for making it. Secondly, the guy that didn't make it has to sit in it a little longer while he hears from men who did make it and he gets to see the fruit of their good choices. Getting the share order right has a powerful effect and gives extra incentive for men to keep from messing up. From a listening perspective, it's nice to hear the good news first before the bad, and then to go straight into prayer time when you do.

HUG

Most men didn't get the physical affection they needed growing up so they end up violating their values to meet a need. Hug each time before you leave and hold on a second longer than is comfortable. The number one love language for men is touch (the Christian way of saying "sex"), and touch meets a huge need, so do it, and do it regularly. The cool part about hugging is that you get one too.

THEIR HEALING IS NOT YOUR RESPONSIBILITY

For most of these men, getting better is just showing up, connecting with other men, and airing out their junk in a place they won't be judged for it. The only real accountability we do is that we expect each man to tell us how he did sexually at the beginning of his time to talk each week. This way we know where he is right away. Knowing he'll have to tell us all how he did with his penis this week right away helps a guy to fight it. Nobody wants to show up and have the first thing out of his mouth be that he did some-

> Jenna's Story: When my husband came to me five years ago and said he wanted to join ManAlive, I was resistant. Him going to group meant he had a problem and everyone was going to find out. I felt ashamed because it meant we didn't have it all together. I knew he had been looking at porn and masturbating about once every three months, he didn't want to make any big decisions for himself or our family, he didn't know how to communicate his heart with me, and he was incredibly passive. But I thought this was just the way life is and the way our marriage was going to be and I was trying to just accept it.
>
> It took him about a year and a half before he got sober and we were beginning to lose hope that anything would ever change. During this time, I finally started opening up with my girlfriends about what we were going through and I was shocked to realize that we weren't the only ones. It was incredibly freeing realizing this, but it also hurt my heart to realize so many women were like me, buried in the shame of their husband's addiction.
>
> When he finally started getting sober from porn and masturbation, I started seeing him truly become a man for the first time. He started pursuing schooling because he finally wasn't afraid to grow. He started opening up his heart to me, weeping on my shoulder from years of holding in pain. He began confronting fears at work and quickly got promoted. He was becoming a man I respected on a deep level.
>
> These huge changes didn't happen all at once, but as they did, we were making more money, having better sex, feeling connected on a level I didn't know was possible, and I was able to use the momentum of our stability to start a business that has been growing exponentially every year.
>
> I've now become a super fan of men's group. Not only am I not ashamed that he goes, but I'm proud to say he's a part of it. I am an evangelist to all my girlfriends, encouraging them that it's exactly what their husbands need. Porn problem or not, every man needs what my husband got at men's group: A chance to become a man.

thing stupid.

Don't be tempted to police a man to sobriety; if you do, it won't last. It's a good thing that policing has no long-term value because it's way too much work. Let the men do the work, and don't work on their problems more than they do. Yes, there is some peer pressure in the small group, but it works only to a point. They have to want it for themselves. The outward discipline of say, not looking at porn, draws out the internal pain that pushed a man to it in the first place.

That pain lets you know you're alive. It is in the place that God heals. If you're feeling pain, you're doing it right. When your men are in pain, it's good, that's what you want. Pain is your friend. It's what they have been trying to avoid, and now that they're in pain you have something to work with because a desperate man in pain is teachable. When a man is in control of his behavior and suffering pain because of it, he's set up for the good things God wants to do.

BE COURAGEOUSLY HONEST

The men in your group are learning how to talk. They are learning how to feel, and so are you. Get naked (figuratively, i.e. emotionally) and be as honest as you know how to be; we are all learning. When you do it, the men in your group will follow you. When Napoleon returned from Elba Island he said, "Strike me down or follow me." His troops followed.

Just keep encouraging your men to be as honest as they can. Be patient, because their "honest as they can" this week will be significantly more honest two months from now. The onion gets peeled down slowly. What's going on in the male mind during this process is the line of thinking that says, "If they knew the real me they wouldn't love me. If they reject me, then I am truly rejected at my core, so I will show them my false self." See the cycle? It's what got them in the room in the first place. So stand up and clap when they say something courageously honest. They will love you for it.

Down and dirty, real, and brutal honesty is their only hope; and no, they can't just do it with God. They must learn to be brutally honest with other men because when they can't feel God, they need someone to touch them. I think God pulls back a bit, ever so slightly, so that we can figure this out and learn our need for others.

Self-hatred has to die. The victim mentality must be killed, no whining allowed. The difference between being honest and complaining is the spirit behind it. If you're complaining, men will pull away from you. If you're being real, they will be drawn to you and love you for it.

I like competition, so I always try to win the most vulnerable contest. We don't have an actual contest for that, but one is unofficially going on all the time. We're men, and yeah, everything is a competition. Create this culture in your group and you will be shocked at how deep you go each week and how quickly your men get better.

ACTIVELY LISTEN

There is a lot going on when you are listening to your men talk. Always remember that everything you do is being watched by the other men, and you are essentially training them in what works and what doesn't. It's on-the-job training and they are quick learners because their penises are very important to them. They're nervous since it's all new to them, so you'll have their full attention. The Holy Spirit is involved and drawing things out because he loves us too much to leave us the way we are. Every situation is different and he will give you insight because you have oversight. So listen to your men with one ear and to the Holy Spirit with the other.

Actively listen. Patton said, "You will be surprised at how much information you can get from someone if you act interested." Sit forward in your chair and look them in the eyes with an open body posture. Don't cross your arms or legs. Don't yawn, look away, exhale, rub your face, or let them catch you looking at your watch. This is their time and they are getting better just by having someone who cares listen to them. This is a first for many and it's exactly what they need.

As you listen to your men each week, collect information and store it. Gather prayer fodder for later. It's super easy to pray for people when you know what to go after. Listen for bad theology and lies that they believe.

SAYING WHAT IS TRUE

During the share, listen for bad theology, wrong thinking, and lies the men in your group believe. When you hear something that is clearly not true address it during the prayer time by doing repeat-after-me statements that say what is true, and you will see a lot of tears. For example, if a man says, "I'm a loser" or "I'm worthless" when he's talking, sometime during the prayer time have him repeat the truth: "I am not a loser" or "I am highly valued." Doing this straightens out what was broken in isolation in a public way and it is powerful. When the lie is spoken, it's broken. Saying it opens them up be loved, valued, and known.

Men will get better incredibly fast when you create an atmosphere where they can process freely without judgment. The freedom that comes with being able to process openly allows us to put words to our thoughts and recognize incorrect thinking when we hear them out loud. Healing takes place many times without a word ever spoken to the man who was sharing.

FIND THE SOURCE OF PAIN

Let's talk about basic psychology. Even though I read a bunch of human psychology books in college, I learned this by working with horses: A man is what he is today because of his past. His past hurts and pains control his future if they are not faced, walked through, and healed. When we were kids we didn't have the tools to face what scared us, but now we are men and we do.

Facing our fears is still super scary, but it's the only option to get better. So listen for traumatic events in your men's pasts that they still carry today and that control what they do now. Trust me, those events are there, these guys didn't just come by their issues genetically; so look for the source of the pain and gently help them get it out and see it for what it is. Putting light on past pain they endured in isolation is healing. Words or prayers aptly spoken into the pain will bring the healing they need to be at peace and to change their future behavior.

Listen for broken relationship structures (for example, with mothers, fathers, peers—both male and female). Are the men giving away to others what they have been receiving? Do they have non-Christian friends? (We need these friendships too.) What hurts and what is missing in their relationships? Help them rebuild what is broken and to make things right with others as much as it's in their power to do so.

ASK FOR HELP

You don't get a sponsor in a small group so each man has to be the friend they would want to have. Have them get other men's phone numbers and call them before they screw up, not after. No one wants to be used as a confessional.

If a man isn't reaching out, ask him why; the majority of men have a tough time with this. One way to teach this is having guys say out loud, "I need help." I can't count how many men have cried over this when I have them do it. Asking for help and accepting help not only hasn't been taught, but we grew up on James Bond and Jason Bourne and it's been subconsciously discouraged. When a guy calls me the first thing I say is, "Good job for making the call. Well done." Then I pray for him. Bam! He wins, you win, and it's all good because he is in the light, the isolation is broken, the connection is made, and the need of his heart is met.

To get out of the cycle of addiction men have to get the needs of their hearts met in a healthy way. This takes time because for the most part they themselves don't know what they need, so there is a long learning curve. Be patient, the rewards are huge, and these guys will love you for it.

MEN AT WORK

Work is a huge part of getting better. It's telling how many men show up who are not working. This group will get them working again. I say things like, "I need you to get twenty job applications out this week, can you do that for me?" If they can't, I ask them not

PART TWO **SMALL GROUP**

Money Stories: One of my favorite things that happens to men who come to group, sober up, and begin to live honestly is that they begin to make money. Men make money when they get themselves out in the light and start doing the work to get better because "whoever conceals his sin does not prosper" (Proverbs 28:13).
There is a spiritual dynamic that is in play here. If you want to prosper stop concealing your sin and live in the open, out in the light, and you will. It's so satisfying for me to watch because men did not come to ManAlive for that purpose—they came to deal with their sin—and the financial side is a bonus.
Men are getting crazy, regular raises at work and just completely killing it with the tools they are learning and now living out in the marketplace. There are mountains of business start-ups too. It's so fun to watch, to be a part of. This stuff is the outward sign of internal transformation.
Joe has been in group four years and has gotten a 20k raise each year he has been in group.
Jeff just had his salary more than doubled as his company created a position for him to manage all the sales on the West Coast. His boss recently commented to him that he has never known anyone who is as humble as he is and yet so confident.
Josh started a construction company that after a few years of struggle is really taking off. He hires almost exclusively men from group and has some fantastic stories of what God is doing in them and through them regularly on the job site.
Kenny couldn't afford the small entry fee we have to get into group. Someone ended up sponsoring him and he has since had several raises and now gets commissions on certain parts of his job. More importantly, for the first time he is living generously.
Mark, after suffering catastrophic financial loss, was reduced to cutting firewood and delivering newspapers for years. He was hired as head of security for a major tech firm in Silicon Valley. His salary compensation that comes with stock is shockingly huge.
Nick, tired of working for someone, quit his job recently and started doing tile at four times what he used to earn. He's so busy, he just hired his first full-time employee.
Casey, whom I have seen struggle for many years at a job with no vacation and after many failed business start-up attempts, started developing products and marketing online, a business that fits him

> perfectly. He has since hired several leaders from group that are building something I am confident will be of great significance.
>
> These are a few of the men in the room. The cool part is that you are next. It might not turn right away, but it will turn. Many times God breaks you down only to set you up, so he can build you up. He is your father, and he wants good things for you, things that you are ready to handle. Right now, wherever you're at in your process, if you're working on the inside of you, the outside will soon follow. One of those outside things I guarantee you, will be you more prosperous than you are now. You have dreams, and dreams take money. Keeping doing the work and soon you'll have both.

to come back. Men are made to protect and provide. If they are not doing that, I bring the heat until they do it or choose to leave.

MANAGING YOU

Listen for how the guys in your group manage themselves. How do they respond when they are emotionally taxed? An acronym to help you judge how they're doing is H.A.L.T.S. Hopeless, Angry, Lonely, Tired, Stressed. Bored should also be in there, but I couldn't make it work in the acronym. Before a man does something stupid he will be feeling at least one of those emotions and many times most of them at once. What are your men doing to combat the things that set them off?

SOME GOOD OPTIONS ARE:
Take a nap; call someone; reduce workload or responsibilities; find something that brings them life; remind themselves what God has said about them.

Teach them how to recognize the things that set them off and to adjust their behavior before they do something dumb that will cement how they are feeling and prolong the agony.

Never condemn failure; men will be hard enough on themselves, trust me, or they wouldn't be in the group. Failure is what you do just before you succeed. So ponder what happened, and go back and see when the slide down the slope started. Help them to see it so they can make adjustments for next time, because there will most likely be a next time. Because you have time with these men, applaud even the slightest improvement. Encouragement is the fuel that propels purity.

HOMEWORK

Push the men in your group with homework each week until they figure out how to give themselves homework. Homework builds momentum by providing opportunities for small victories, which lay a foundation of success to build on. Momentum is crucial. Every man is tempted, but an idle man tempts the devil. Make sure the guys in your group are always working on something. The second thing out of each man's mouth each week, right after how he did sexually, should be how he did with his homework.

HERE ARE SOME EXAMPLES OF GOOD HOMEWORK:
1. Call three people this week and hang out with one of them outside the group.
2. Take a hike to a lake or waterfall and when you get there take a swim.
3. Go to sleep by 10 p.m.
4. Take your guitar out in the woods and worship.
5. Go fishing.
6. Cut out something that is dragging you down this week (for example, internet, video games, alcohol, or Facebook).
7. Make some small step toward pursuing a dream this week.
8. Break off an unhealthy relationship or reestablish contact with an old friend.

Homework is identifying a problem and then giving something to do about it. If a man is out of work, his homework is to get out twenty job applications this week. If a man doesn't do his homework one week, I'll let it slide with the warning that if he doesn't do it next week he doesn't get to share. Don't worry too much about giving the perfect homework, just give some. A man needs movement, momentum. He needs to take action. Here is a categorized list of examples of homework I've given in the past.

PHYSICAL FITNESS AND HEALTH
- Thirty-minute cardio workout three times a week.
- Brush your teeth, comb your hair, put on deodorant, shave or trim and wear clean clothes every day.
- Wash your car, clean your house, make your bed, fix everything that's broken, sell what you don't need.
- Wax your car and change the oil in your car.
- Cut wood in the summer time.
- Get your teeth cleaned.
- Take a family hike.
- Don't go out to any restaurants or buy any prepackaged food for a set period of time.
- Eat organic food only this week.
- Stop drinking sodas.
- Don't eat anything that's not the way God created it.
- Plant something.

TRAINING NEW HABITS
- Don't cross your arms or legs, make eye contact with everyone while they are speaking.
- Plan ahead.
- Don't spend any money this month except on gas and food at the grocery store.
- Don't go out to any restaurants or buy any prepackaged food.
- Buy yourself some good shoes.
- Get ten books at the library on something that interests you, read two of them and skim the rest.
- Offend five people this week on purpose.
- Go to an AA meeting.
- Attend a worship service at another church.
- Go to the synagogue in town.
- Tell someone something you've never told anyone.
- Compliment three people everyday this week.
- Tell five people this week about something they do that bothers you.
- Do three random acts of kindness.
- Help someone old, someone your age, and someone younger than you this week.
- Wait one month before you buy anything you want and then spend another month looking for it on Craigslist before you pull the trigger.
- Stop drinking alcohol.
- Stand up to your parents.
- Stop saying the words "hot girl," "hot babe," or "hot chick" and replace them with "beautiful woman" or nothing at all.
- No social media, Netflix, YouTube, etc. for the week or for an indefinite period of time.
- Go to bed by 10 p.m. every night and wake up at a certain time. Get right out of bed.
- What are you afraid of? Do that.

RELATIONSHIP
- Make eye contact with everyone while they are speaking to you.
- Take your wife out to a nice dinner and get a babysitter.
- Invite friends over for dinner.
- Take a family hike.
- Compliment three people every day this week.

PART TWO SMALL GROUP

- Join a sports team, preferably something masculine like jujitsu, boxing, wrestling, football, or rugby.
- Make dinner for your family and clean it up.
- Pick up the lunch tab for a friend and fill someone's gas tank.
- Help someone old, someone your age, and someone younger than you this week.
- Write a list of reasons you proposed to your wife.
- No social media, Netflix, YouTube, etc. for the week or for an indefinite period of time.
- Call your mom or dad.
- Talk to your roommate about that thing he did that bothered you.
- Come back to group next week ready to tell us something you've never told anyone before.

ADVENTURE
- Take a massive road trip or head into the wilderness.
- Hunt, kill, and eat a deer, fish, or shellfish.
- Join a sports team, preferably something masculine like jujitsu, boxing, wrestling, football, or rugby.
- Sleep outside.
- Build a fire outside and cook something over it.
- Cut wood in the summer.
- Cut down a tree with an axe.
- Dig your own worms and go fishing with them.
- Go skinny-dipping.
- Take a dump in the woods.
- Take a family hike.
- Jump off a bridge, climb a mountain, go fishing, work on your song, kill something.
- What are you afraid of? Do that.

RESPONSIBILITY
- Learn to take care of something other than yourself. Buy a pet.
- Plant a garden, raise or hatch some chickens.
- Store up for the future. Buy quality food when it's on sale and freeze it.
- Save some money.
- Wash your car, clean your house, make your bed, fix everything that's broken, sell what you don't need.
- Wax your car and change your oil.
- Cut wood in the summer.
- Start a business.
- Go to an AA meeting.
- Invite friends over for dinner.
- Plant something.
- Make dinner for your family and clean it up.
- Wait one month before you buy anything you want and then spend another month looking for it on Craigslist before you pull the trigger.
- Stop drinking alcohol.
- List four business ideas you can do right now with what you have available to you.
- Stand up to your parents.
- Write a list of reasons you proposed to your wife.
- Come to group on time.
- Go to bed by 10 p.m. every night and wake up at a certain time. Get right out of bed.

Homework confronts passivity. It shocks, attacks, and brings action to idleness, procrastination, laziness, and avoidance. Homework does something about the problem. One of the most common traits in an addicted man is passivity. Passive men are always looking for someone else to make their decisions, fight

> Steve's Story: I've been married for ten years. I have three amazing kids. I'm from Australia and I've spent a third of my life struggling with the issue of sexual purity. Before coming to Redding, I was a pastor and often spoke to guys around Australia on the topic of purity. I knew firsthand how much of a hidden struggle it was for every male in the church—feeling isolated and alone. I would empower men to own it and often express it for the first time. But I had no idea how to bring the tools to walk men into full freedom.
>
> There is a big difference between confession and repentance, and actually living in freedom. That was me. For years I had learned how to white knuckle (meaning: just try really hard not to go back to the counterfeit comforts, such as porn, masturbation, food, alcohol, whatever it is to help relieve the stress of life), but I never felt free or pure. The shame caused me to disconnect from all those closest to me—my wife, kids and God.
>
> We have a saying in ManAlive that porn, like alcohol, overeating or any other counterfeit comfort is merely the check engine light that tells us that there is something wrong with the engine of our heart. It's like referral pain—you get a numbness or pain, say in your hand, but the issue is actually stemming way back up to a pinched nerve or an inability to feel somewhere else. Porn isn't the problem, it's the tell sign that something else is broken. ManAlive gave me not only the space and encouragement to work on my heart issues but equipped me with the tools I needed to fix them.
>
> Getting really honest with myself on a daily basis, going deeper and deeper into areas that caused me pain, and learning how to find and sustain relationships with people who I could share my deepest stuff with helped me break through into a whole new level of freedom that I never knew was available.
>
> I remember the day the realization dropped on how far I had actually come. I was about to take communion—I always take it so seriously—and as I stopped to reflect on my past few weeks, I couldn't think of a single thing that I needed to confess or was ashamed of. For the first time in my life I felt the power of God's holiness and I stopped and wept. I'd never felt so free.

their battles and ultimately for someone else to make them better. Homework is an act of humility. If they don't choose to humble themselves, then they can't be helped. It's also an act of war. Homework puts the sword in their hands, it gives them a goal along with a cheering section. Homework = healing.

EAT TOGETHER

If you want to be a great leader, feed your men. Men love food. The Alpha Course expanded all over the world and revived the Anglican church because their people ate together. Eating together is communion. It's intimate. You take food into your body and you share it with others. It feels good; it's family. So when you meet outside of the room, make sure there is food. Provide good food; don't ever bring a lame lamb to a sacrifice. The men will catch on to this good-food thing after a while and start asking what they can bring, and that is a good sign. Giving to others is one of the steps in getting free.

***

Some of you men are a little nervous to lead a group. That's okay; let that energy work for you. You will rise to the occasion and leading will get you better faster than sitting in a group. It will help you articulate what's only rolled around in your head before. When Patton flew into North Africa to take over control of all the U.S. and Allied forces on the ground he said, "A man's spirit enlarges with responsibility." Yours will too.

These are the basics. Use them, refine them, and make them your own. Educate yourself. Some great books are *Falling Forward, Breaking Free, Wild at Heart, War as I Knew It,* and my favorite, *ManAlive*.[4] Let me remind you again to be focused on getting better yourself and always asking yourself, "Would I want to go to this group?" If the answer is yes, you're doing it right.

---

4. *Falling Forward: The Pursuit of Sexual Purity* by Craig Lockwood, *Breaking Free: Understanding Sexual Addiction & the Healing Power of Jesus* by Russell Willingham, *Wild at Heart: Discovering the Secrets of a Man's Soul* by John Eldredge, and *War as I Knew It* by General George Patton.

3
GO BIG

NO MATTER HOW HARD YOU TRY TO KEEP THE GROUP QUIET, if you're doing it right, you won't be able to. Men that are getting sexually free and experiencing intimacy, friendship, love, and acceptance can't shut up because they are so happy. So be prepared to grow. Begin with the end in mind, and have a men's group that's so good it will make men love to come to church. We have that with our group, and this section tells how we did it. It's how we still do it. Yours will look different, because you're you, but learn from us then go get it done. If you have the hearts of the men, you have the hearts of the church. If we can get that right, we'll change the world.

Much of what I write on this subject is meant to get men in a small group. Do not be distracted by the many good books, websites, conferences, videos, and speakers out there. If they do not push men into consistent, honest, intimate relationships then they hold little long-term value.

A lot of good, well-intentioned things start with a charismatic man that can bring people together and fill a room with bodies. After that everybody looks around and starts scratching their heads because it lacks community and they're lonely. John Wimber said, "People come to church for many reasons, they stay because they make friends." When you can grab the vision of what this group will look like in five, ten, or twenty years it will propel you forward toward capturing a level of intimacy that few have ever had. When you experience it, it will hook you.

Gabriella's Story: My husband and I had been married for six years and our marriage had become pretty rocky. We had both brought all of our past pain into the marriage, and had become pros at making each other feel awful. We were at the end of our rope, coping in unhealthy ways, and even questioning if we could keep going. That summer I asked God to help our marriage, and within weeks, my husband told me he was joining ManAlive.

It was only a few months into men's group when he started changing. He was coming home on Monday nights, happy. He was crying and dealing with his pain at group, but strangely enough, that was making him happy. He would be watching a movie with me, and the next thing you know, he'd be in the fetal position on my lap sobbing. I knew it was a deep and holy work of the Lord, and I just tried to pray over him quietly, hold him, and let God do His work. Most of the time he didn't talk, and I didn't know what was going on exactly, but I knew he was grieving deep pain that he had carried for a long time. It was a beautiful and holy season with the Lord, and it was lifting heaviness off of him.

Every week he was getting better! He was calling his friends, and getting together for coffee or lunch. Soon, it wasn't just Mondays that he was happy, but Monday and Tuesday, then Monday through Thursday, and so on, until he was just happy. Even during that year and half season when he was actively grieving pain, he was simultaneously happy. Every time he cried it was as if another weight fell off and he could stand up a little straighter and smile a little bigger. He was getting free, and long-buried places in his heart were coming alive again.

He began doing things he loved again: photography, kayaking, treasure hunting, and growing a sexy beard, to name a few. It was like I married this great guy, and surprise, he's even greater than I thought! Score!

Well, you know the phrase happy wife, happy life? I now say, happy husband, happy family. I tell him all the time that he is the most important person in our family, and I truly believe that. He is the one who leads and inspires me, and I am able to give that strength to our children. He makes me feel like we matter, like we are going somewhere important, and are a part of a magical journey!

As I watched him get better, I jumped on board, wanting more healing and freedom too. I didn't have group to walk me through it, so, I just decided to go after it myself. Honestly, I just started copying

> him. I prayed and went back into old painful memories with the Holy Spirit, and just cried through them. It was like God was rewriting my stories and my husband was there to hold me as I cried, and pray over me, too. We healed together and forgave each other along the way, and grew in love and friendship.
>
> As a result of our healing and growth through ManAlive, our marriage has gotten better and better! We are more connected and in love than ever, and truly champion each other every day. Now, we are expecting our fourth child and have nothing but joy and excitement for the future. ManAlive has been the most important thing that we have ever been a part of, and it has completely changed our lives.

ManAlive is church planting inside the church; it's a man-making machine, and if you're doing it right, you get to multiply yourself, over, and over, and over again. When you start it right, it gets easier as you grow, not harder. It doesn't look too sexy to start with a small group of broken men, but if you can see the future you become David at the Cave of Adullam with those who are in distress, in debt, and bitter of soul.[1] Those same broken men expanded the kingdom of Israel more than anyone before or after and became the greatest army in biblical history. David did it, and he did it with the broken.

We just had the tenth anniversary of our men's group and we have never missed a meeting, holidays and all. This year Monday falls on Christmas and New Year's Day, and yes, we'll meet then too. God will show up, his presence will be felt. Men will weep and go home better. To do this thing is an all in game. Don't try to do it half way, or a watered-down, socially acceptable version of it. When men come with a problem they come humble and teachable, and then, they become powerful.

Strongly resist the temptation to make an announcement and have a big kick off. If you do, a bunch of men show up, you will have no leaders and without them you have nothing. Build it slow, build it right, and it will outlast your lifetime. The fruit of the

---

1. 2 Sam 22:1.

men's lives that come through the doors will affect generations to come—an incalculable reward.

Here you go. You've started your first group nice and quietly, just like Jesus. It's undercover. It's slowly growing. Men are getting better. You are getting better, people are catching wind of what is going on. They want what you have. They start to show up. They want in.

You have a couple of guys that are doing great. They're ready to lead, and you know it's time. You'll know you're right when the men coming in match the leaders that you have ready. God is with you. (I have to take a commercial break here to tell you the miracle we've experienced over and over again. For a decade straight we have never had more men that want to join than we've had leaders ready to lead. We have had more leaders than men wanting to join, but usually not for long. Men just keep showing up when we have the leaders ready. It's beautiful. It's humbling. It's God.)

Here is where it starts to get fun. You've done the hardest work of all by starting that first group. It's all downhill from here. Not that it won't be hard, but you'll like it because you're in the messy mix of men growing and getting better, of lives being changed.

GROWING BEYOND ONE SMALL GROUP

When you're just starting, only meet for one hour, and only do small group with a very brief talk that's under five minutes long. There are a lot of ways to manage your group's growth. Here are some suggestions that work. The day you grow to eight men, split the group and give the new group to the best man you have. (We choose group leaders who are sober, committed, employed, have the ability to lead, and most importantly have a relationship with Jesus.)

Once you split and have two small groups, everything starts to change and the fun really begins. Now when you meet start off with both groups together, do a short talk, and share testimonies before you go to small group. Good news shared corporately keeps the unity of the whole.

As men keep coming add them to the split groups until they reach seven men each. When these groups are full, again pick out your best man and start another group. The momentum of growth is fun to watch and be a part of. To grow well takes time and really comes down to developing great leaders. When I'm talking to other ManAlive leaders around the world, I don't ask how many men they have. I ask how many leaders they have, and that tells me what I need to know.

When you hit three groups, pull out the guitar. Keep worship short, maybe just a couple of simple songs (just enough for the men to get their hearts centered in the right place) and keep having a short talk and doing testimonies. As the group grows, slowly increase the time allotted for each segment. Games should be added to the schedule last.

The following is a breakdown of how we run our group. Please adapt it and make it your own. This is what we've found works for us after many mistakes, failings, and adjustments.

We meet at 7 p.m. on Mondays—that's every Monday, holidays and all. Our general format goes like this:
- Worship: 20 minutes with a short opener and closer.
- Game or Contest: 10 minutes.
- Testimonies: 5 minutes.
- Speaker: 30 minutes.
- Small Group: 45 minutes to 1 hour.

I strongly suggest that men who have not attended ManAlive here in Redding or one of our affiliate groups join one of our online groups before starting your own small group. You'll get better, and you will learn how small group is done from a man who is good at it. Also, and this is very important, you will establish a relationship with your group leader and gain a mentor along the way so you have someone to call to work through problems and ask questions—someone to cheer you on. For more information and to join up, go to imanalive.com. It's critical for your success and for the men that come to your group that you do this. It's a short six-month commitment that will pay you back many, many times over. This is a great book that outlines what to do and why we do it, but to do it right, to do it well, you need to taste the atmosphere, experience the fruit, and receive the love. You'll get all of that and more in the online group.

WORSHIP

We worship just long enough for men to get their heads in the right place. Worship, if we're doing it right, brings us face to face with the living God. It peels away the junk from the day and gets us focused on Jesus. It creates expectancy in the room and in our hearts, reminding us that we're not in this alone. He is there to help us, save us, heal us.

We sing two or sometimes three simple songs that we all know in a key we can really belt out loud. I like songs that aren't too wordy, songs that have the word "holy" or "Jesus," songs that connect us with our deep need and desperation for him, songs that make us feel like men. I'm not looking for songs about God, but rather for songs that we sing to him. Songs that remind us who he is, what he has done, and what he is about to do.

I want a worship leader who brings us into the presence of God. I don't particularly care as much how musically talented he is, although that is nice. I do very much care how anointed he is. Some of the most anointed worship leaders are some of the most broken men in the room.

Desperate worship is great worship. Worship is warfare and worshipers get well because worship is a relational act of intimacy with God; sexual sin is a counterfeit to that intimacy. Worship is the center of our relationship with God. When we worship well, we get well.

PART THREE GO BIG

Pete's Story: For most of my life, if someone would have asked me to articulate the area in my life that brought me the most shame and felt the most emasculating, the first thing to come to mind would have been my decades-long struggle with porn and masturbation. I thought living in sexual purity required either a transformational miracle or an unbreakable will of iron.

Several years ago I walked into ManAlive for the first time and heard what seemed to be the most confident man in the world speaking about something I had never even admitted to myself was possible—the idea that God calls us to embark on a lifelong journey toward complete and authentic freedom, where each day is lived better and more freely than the previous day.

Mark didn't speak about a divine quick fix or pass along self-help techniques, he painted a picture of men living with purpose and in communion with Jesus and each other, with sexual purity arising out of the overflow of their hearts coming fully alive. I happily paid the entrance fee to join one of the small groups that night.

Being in ManAlive has had an impact on every aspect of who I am and how I live: the way I think, the way I feel, the way I view myself, the way I make decisions, the way I pursue and connect with my wife, the way I love my kids, the way I connect with the heart of the Father.

I've learned that freedom in sexual purity is neither an unattainable ideal nor is it a static state of being. Rather, it's an unending journey of vulnerability, of assertiveness, of men truly becoming who God has called us to be.

About a month ago I looked my wife in the eyes and told her that there was nobody on the planet I would rather have sex with than her. This may seem like a basic statement coming from a married man, but it was a significant moment for me. There's no way I would have been able to say this with every single bit of my heart fully present just a few years ago. We're coming up on our ninth year of marriage, but this is the year where it feels like we're finally starting to get sex right. My heart has never felt fuller than it does today but here's the most remarkable thing: I know tomorrow will be even better.

Gideon tore down the Asherah pole that belonged to his father and in the same place built an alter of worship.[2] He then led one of the greatest revivals in biblical history. Asherah poles were ancient pornography, carved wooden images of breasts and genitalia. He got rid of his dad's porn. He turned from his father's sin and replaced it with a place of worship.

Worship is crucial to our healing. It invites the presence of God that transforms lives. Great moves of God happen, both personally and corporately, when we purpose ourselves to worship. Above all else men, make worship a priority. When it's done well, we get well.

GAMES

This is big fun. Men love to compete. The day they stop competing, they're dead. A contest brings men to life, but there is deeper purpose in why we do what we do. Some games are physical and showcase talent or stamina like the one-handed push-up contest, the chair jump, or the hold your breath in a bucket of water contest. Other games get us over fear of rejection because we have to look stupid or show a side of ourselves or a talent we have that others would not have known about without the game. Some of our games work on working together like the bat relay, dodgeball, or the blindfolded chicken catching contest. Men get to enjoy the camaraderie of getting dirty together to achieve a goal. They have to communicate, strategize, and encourage one another. Games connect us to others. But more than anything they're fun. We laugh, slap high fives, and cheer wildly. We're men. Win or lose, it's beautiful because it's relational.

Another important function of the games we play is to recapture what was lost. Many men missed a lot of innocent fun growing up because they were preoccupied with sex, so they are emotionally underdeveloped. When we play a game later in life that we missed

2. Judges 6–7.

playing in junior high because we were chasing girls or porning out, it brings healing.

We always give away a prize. Napoleon said that if he would have had enough medals, he could have taken over the world. It's amazing what a man will do to win something. We have given away a lot of different things over the years but hands down, men like to win food. When food is the prize, the winner can eat it right now and share the spoils with his friends. I like to go with a box of cookies, donuts, a nice craft beer on occasion, or a gift card to In-N-Out Burger for first place. The second place prize is usually a small bag of chocolate of some variety, and third place is almost always a banana. Sometimes, I'll have another banana to give away as a consolation prize to the guy who wiped out the hardest, got the dirtiest, tried extra hard, or just made me laugh.

One limiting factor for a lot of games is time. Five to seven minutes is where you want to land, but no more than ten. I really like playing dodgeball, but a couple of games will eat up twenty minutes. But we still need to play it, so it's a once a year thing. I do dodgeball on a night I'm speaking and shorten my talk. Some things are important to do even if they are long, but generally I'm working real hard to keep it short. You can have a good laugh and a lot of fun in ten minutes.

When it works, play music that matches the contest. I like "I Get Around" by the Beach Boys for the bat relay, or "Eye of the Tiger" for the push-up contest. I listen to mostly country, so that is usually what I play. It gets guys pumped up and sets the mood, making the experience that much better.

Sexual purity groups have this dark-church-basement reputation. Forget that, we're having fun out in the sunshine. We're fearless. Games bring the cool to the misconceptions.

Here are some of the games we play, how we play them, and why. We've done a bunch more but these are some of our best, tried and true, and very fun. They are listed in groups: physical, vulnerable, developmental, and relational. And they're all just plain fun. Rotate the category of game from week to week to let different guys with different talent levels have a chance to win.

PHYSICAL PROWESS AND CONTESTS OF STRENGTH

Push-up or Sit-up Contest. A variation is the one-handed push-up contest. Have everyone start together. Each man has a counter who puts his fist on the ground to make sure the player goes down low enough to touch the counter's fist with his chest. On the sit-up competition, we have the players do sit-ups at a steep angle, using the stairs to the stage, so they're really hard to do. The counter holds the player's feet. For the one-handed push-ups, I let the players switch hands one time. I am regularly amazed at how many one-handed push-ups these guys can do. It's a respect thing in the room for sure.

Breath Holding Contest. Get some five gallon buckets, fill them almost full with water and line them up. The men competing should get on their knees and stick their faces up to just before their ears in the water (so they can hear). Count off in fifteen-second intervals and also let them know how many men are left so each player knows where he stands. It gets pretty cool near the end as everyone is yelling out encouragement.

Chair Jump. Line up three chairs and get as many volunteers as you can. Give the guys a big running start and keep adding one chair to the line after everyone clears it. You'll have some great wipeouts and loud cheering.

Hot Dog, Banana, Onion, Bread, Cinnamon, Lemon, Gold Fish, Raw Trout, or Watermelon Eating Contest. These are a big hit with the single guys in the room. Plus they get free food. A fun way to get guys to eat a bunch of crazy stuff is to play a game show. Get four guys up front, ask them questions that have to do with group. If they know the answer they hit a buzzer. If they're right, they get points. If they're wrong, they eat a surprise out of the bag. Love this game.

Water Bottle Grab. Get some empty water bottles and pile them up on one side of the room. Line up the men who want to play on the other side and have one less water bottle than there are men playing each time. When you say go, the guys playing run and grab a bottle. It turns into a big dog pile and is super funny. Whoever doesn't come up with a bottle is out. Keep removing one bottle and eliminate one guy each time you go. Mix it up a little bit by changing the way they can go get the bottle, like hop on one leg, crawl, roll, or run backward.

Frozen T-Shirt. Get a bunch of t-shirts from a garage sale, wad them up, and freeze them inside one gallon zip lock bags full of water. Go out in the parking lot, give each guy a hammer. First guy to bust it out, put the shirt on and then rip it off wins. Make sure to film this one so you can laugh again each time you watch it.

VULNERABILITY GAMES

These games push all kinds of insecurity buttons because they can make us look dumb in front of people. Just getting up there in front of everyone is a risk that leads to getting better. These games show something about ourselves that risks rejection because we have to show other men a part of who we are that few have ever seen.

Hairy Chest Contest. A variation is the Hairy Back Contest. Another good one is the Who Has the Least Amount of Hair Contest. Get a line of guys up front and have them take off their shirts one at a time to the applause of the room. The winner will be obvious and crowd response is the best part of the game.

Dance Contest. This is one of my all-time favorites and we have several different ways we do it. One way is to get some guys up front and play a three-minute montage of popular dance songs from each decade. Another way that will get some great laughs is to have each player pick a song he wants to dance to, then tell everyone the song and put earphones on the dancer so he can hear the music but everyone else can't. Hilarious. Another good one is to just have them say the song they are going to dance to but not play any music, so it's just one guy at a time, cold on the stage singing the music in his head and dancing. Super funny. Air guitar is another form of dance contest that's a huge hit as well. Just get a bunch of guys up in front and play something with a great guitar solo and let them go at it. It's a great laugh.

Twenty Second Talking Contest. I like games that have something to do with what we're learning in the room. It helps to sell the game and get guys up to play. I'll even invent games along these lines. I came up with this game because learning to talk is such a big deal. Get a bunch of random subjects, write them down on little pieces of paper, and put them in a hat. Each man has a turn to draw one out and read it. Once he hears the word, he has five seconds to prepare, then twenty seconds to talk about how sexual purity relates to it. It's so funny. The last guy I remember who won had the word "French Toast." Applaud for the winner at the end.

Screaming Contest. Go down to the thrift shop and buy a bunch of t-shirts so guys can rip them off as they scream as loud as they can. The best Tarzan yell is a good one too. You might show a video of Tarzan yelling in the jungle to get them inspired.

Body Building Contest. Once you get the guys up front, have them take off their shirts and rub on some baby oil. Then play some funky 70s music while they flex their muscles. This is a riot. The best built guys never win this game. It's the performance that gets the applause. Great laughs too.

Singing Contests. Give each man fifteen to twenty seconds to sing a song of his pick, no music. You'll be surprised and deeply moved at how good men sing. They don't even have to sing well, it's just that they did it. There won't be much, if any, laughter but there will be a lot of applause. It's great. For great laughs do a singing contest called **iPod Idol**. Each player picks a song from the list, then puts the earphones on to sing it. He thinks he's singing great, but it's very often way off tune. Plus he's up there dancing to the music while he sings it. Hilariously huge laughs. Barbershop quartet competitions are fun too. One of the best singing games is **Sing Song Ping Pong**. Get a bunch of guys up front. Split them into two equal groups, pick a song to start out with, and flip a coin to decide which team goes first. Each man has fifteen seconds to sing the chorus of a song with the teams rotating back and forth singing. The fun comes in because each song must relate to the last song sung in some way. So if one team sang "Row Row Row Your Boat," a song that would relate is "Michael Row Your Boat Ashore" and so on. Each man on the team has to go once. He can get help deciding which song to sing while the other team is singing, but he must sing the song himself. Players on his team can be backup singers and dancers for extra points. Winner is awarded by applause, great game.

Tattoo contest. Each man playing has twenty seconds to tell us about his tattoo—when and why he got it, and what it means to him. This is a very cool game. I don't have a tattoo myself, but what we've learned about the men in the room through this game went deep. A similar game is the scar contest. Each man playing has thirty seconds to tell the story behind the scar. For both these games, the winner is determined by applause.

DEVELOPMENTAL GAMES

These are what you missed out on as a kid and we're recapturing that which was lost. These games are mostly pretty dumb, but they're awfully fun.

Blindfolded Shoe Hunt. Have about ten guys or so take off their shoes. Put the shoes in a pile. Then move the players about twenty yards away. Have them close their eyes and race to find their own shoes. When they put their shoes back on, they then have to go jump into an assigned person's arms (this person is hiding in the room somewhere) to win. The big laughs happen when there is a pile of guys wrestling over a pile of shoes.

The Big Swinging Cucumber. You need empty soda cans, string, and cucumbers. Tie the string around each player's waist and tie the cucumber to the other end of the string so it is hanging straight down between his legs. The object is to use the swinging cucumber to knock the empty soda can along the ground across the finish line that is about thirty yards away. Play some music while they do it. Big fun.

Eating Live Fish Bait. This is always a huge hit. We've done a bunch of different styles of play with this game—the best one we call, **Mother Hen.** Guys come up and flap their arms like wings and say, "cheep, cheep," like they are baby birds and want food to eat. Then we grab something that is a total surprise to them out of the bag and feed it to them. Start slow and build up. Go with a raw egg first, then a night crawler, a grub, a live minnow, and finish with a crayfish. The crowd will go wild with amusement. Have a trash can nearby in case anyone needs to puke.

Drink a Soda Through a Sock. You can do it with clean socks, their own socks, or if you're feeling more adventurous, have them put their own sock over the can and at the last moment have them switch cans so they have to drink through someone else's sock. There will be a collective moan and lots of laughing from the crowd. Very fun.

Eat a Cookie Off Your Forehead. This is a good quick game that gets a good laugh. Have whoever wants to play sit in a line of chairs with their heads tilted back. Place a large cookie on each of their foreheads. They have to eat the cookie without it falling to the ground and without using their hands. I'll put a bonus piece of candy on top of the cookie sometimes and say if you get candy and eat the cookie first and win, I'll give you twenty dollars. It's nearly impossible, but I've seen it done and paid the twenty to thunderous applause.

High Heel Hurdles. Get a bunch of high heel shoes without the back, or cut the backs off. Set up an obstacle course with short hurdles, two-by-fours to walk across, cones to weave through, and hula hoops to jump to on the ground. Duct tape the shoes to each player's feet and have a race. The guy who won last year was the biggest guy that played with giant calves and feet. Hysterical.

Stuff a Car. Find the guy with the smallest car. Line everyone up that wants to play from biggest to smallest then number them off ones and twos so that each team has guys that are of equal size. The team that fits the most guys in the car wins. I recommend taking off shoes, and the rearview mirror. The car gets packed so tight that the last two times we've played, we've broken the front windshield. Last time we stuffed fifteen men into a Geo Metro, that has to be some kind of record. It's great.

Donut on a String. Get a board or a broom handle and tie twelve strings to it. Then get a dozen donuts and tie them on the hanging end of each string. The strings should be close enough that the donuts barely touch. Have two men hold up the broom handle. This is a donut eating contest and you can't use your hands or drop the donut. Play some music while the players eat and have a good laugh while they smash donuts all over each other's faces. You might bring some wipes or paper towels too.

Naked Man Musical Chairs. It's musical chairs with a twist. Have those playing put their shirts and pants on a chair so they're just in their boxers. The players walk around the circle of chairs and when the music stops they have to put on whatever clothes are on the chair as fast as they can and sit down. Last guy down is out. Keep going till you have a winner. The comedy here is the off-size of the clothes guys have to put on.

Inch Worm. Have the guys who want to play strip down to their boxers and wrap them each in cellophane as tightly as you can with their feet together and arms by their sides. Then lay them in a line and put a banana on a plate for each player about twenty yards away. The players have to inch their way, like a worm, over to the banana and eat it. First one done wins. You will laugh hard.

RELATIONAL OR TEAM GAMES

These are great for connecting guys. These games break isolation and get us talking. They teach us to work together and get us close to people. It's more fun to win together.

Tug-O-War. Have all the men take off their shirts. Then split the room in half by hairy chests versus non-hairy chests. We do this every year and I have been on the no hair side. No hair is up two to one.

Dodgeball. You know what to do. For the sake of time don't let anyone come back in the game. Once you're out of the game, you're out. Ways to split the room are by odd or even birthdays, or by young guys versus the old guys.

Bat Relay. Get in teams relay style. One guy from each team runs about forty yards or so, picks up a baseball bat, and spins around ten times with his head on the bat and the bat touching the ground. Have a counter for each team count each spin out loud. The fun starts when the players try to run back to their lines. Because they're so dizzy there are a lot of great wipeouts. Keep going until everyone in the line has had a turn. Another version of this I call **Drunken Sailor.** The game is the same except instead of spinning looking down, they have to put the bat on their chin and look up. This gets you way dizzier. Then when running back to their team they have to walk the plank across the bodies of all the guys in their team, who are lying face down in a single file line on the floor. Not one guy could do it the first time. If you fall off the plank, you have to drop down, do five push-ups and start again. Super funny, super fun.

Football Toss. I like to do this one around Super Bowl time. Each guy playing gets a partner. One partner stands on the stage or up high on something; he should put his ankles together and stand bowlegged. The other partner, from about twenty yards out, tries to throw the football between his legs. He gets extra points if the ball passes through close to his partner's tenders. Yes, someone usually gets hit there . . . .

Goat Milk Relay. I have some milk goats, so I bring a couple of them for this game. Have teams line up in relay lines. Players have to run down to the goats and lie on their backs while a teammate squirts milk straight from the goat into their mouths. When the player's mouth is full he has to run back and spit the milk into a cup. The team who fills its cup first wins. I wish I would have taken a picture of all the shocked faces the first time I did this. The guys got through the shock and it has been one of our best games ever.

Blindfolded Chicken Catching Contest. This is my all-time favorite game. All you need is a chicken; a rooster is preferable. Find a small fenced area. We use one that is about fifty by fifty feet that works perfectly. Let the chicken go in the fenced area. Have each man playing get a partner. One guy is blindfolded and the other is following right behind him (without touching him) telling him where to go and how to catch the chicken. I'm not sure how I came up with this game, but the first time we did it I laughed until my stomach hurt. The chicken naturally moves away from people; like a good running back he'll even shoot the gaps and go into the open area. All the guys playing look really slow as they grab for a chicken that is not there. Not to fear though, participants usually figure it out in a few minutes, holding the bird up to loud cheers.

Cheetos Feet Feed. Get a bag of big Cheetos and some paper plates. Have the men playing grab a partner. Count out ten Cheetos for each team and put them on a plate. One guy lies down and the other, with his bare feet, feeds him five Cheetos. When he's done with the five, they switch places. First team done wins. It is awkwardly funny to watch guys with toe lint try to get a Cheeto in the other guy's mouth. You will laugh.

Balloon Battle. Split into two teams. Each man ties one balloon to one ankle with about three feet of string. Now try to pop the all the balloons on the other team using only your feet. Balloons should all be blown up to be the same size. If your balloon pops, you're out. The last team standing wins. A cool variation is to have three guys on the team with a different colored balloon and the last team standing with one of these balloons wins. It's fun because a bunch of strategy comes into play in the protection of those three guys, and in the attacks on the other team. Another good team battle game is to have a rubber band war. Go buy a giant bag of rubber bands, split into teams, five rubber bands per man. If you get hit on the body, you're out, last team standing wins. We have also played the same game with Nerf darts and PVC pipes. The pipes were cut two feet long for blowing the darts out like a blow gun. Very fun.

This list is far from exhaustive, but you get the idea. I keep a running list (it's up to 150) of games we've played with a one to ten ranking system. If I'm not getting any fresh ideas for a game that night, I go to my list, skim it and look for games we haven't played in a while with a nine or ten ranking so I know I have a winner.

Use what works for you and make up your own. The main point is that men like to play, get scratched up, and get dirty. They look forward to the game each week. It's more than an ice-breaker. It brings us to life, gets us into real time, and gets our blood pumping.

Keep the games short and shocking. Praise the winner and encourage the guys who had the courage to get up front and make fools of themselves. We heal better together and it's healthy for a man to blow off steam. A lot of the time, guys are just stuck, and winning can give them a good lift. I have noticed over the years that the men who get up front and play the most games are often the men who get better faster.

When doing a game, I explain what we're going to do and what the rules are. Then I show off the prize and explain the criteria for winning. In the physical or team games, the winner is usually clear. But in the vulnerable or developmental games, it's subjective, so the winner is determined by applause. If there were twenty guys in the screaming contest, I would bring up the top three to five guys at the end and have a scream off and then ask all the guys in the audience to cheer for their favorite.

To start a game I call for volunteers. If I don't get enough, I keep selling it until I do. If we're playing a game that's a little scary and we're still short then I will hit them with, "There's method in my madness men. There is a reason we're playing this game. It's for you to get better on the inside, and now is your chance." I tell them David, a man after God's own heart, danced in his jockstrap in front of the whole city and teenage girls. He did it, you can do it too. Often the same guys will want to come up each week, which is fine, but I might discourage them on occasion just to have some new blood up there. Every now and then I'll say only the guys who have never played a game can play this one, just to break new guys out of their shells.

TESTIMONIES

Testimonies should be short, one minute, maybe two if we're all crying. They should be brief, honest, and in a natural, no church words type of way—what we're looking for in one minute or less is: "This is where I was. This is where I am now. This is how I got there."

The primary function of the testimony is to release hope: "Wow, that guy did it and he was really screwed up. If he did it, I can do it too." Testimonies say if God did it once, he'll do it again. When the men tell fresh stories of getting better, week after week, the faith in the room rises. It's like fishing when everyone around you is catching fish. You start looking to see what bait they're using. How are they doing it? You start to fish confidently, and you start to catch fish too.

Testimonies can be dangerous if you don't clearly outline what the guidelines are each time before you start. It usually goes something like this: "OK, it's time for testimonies. To give a testimony you have to have been in the room for three months or more, and it needs to have something to do with you getting better or something to do with your penis, in one minute or less. Who's got one?"

What I'm looking for is the fruit of what they are growing into, what they're learning. I don't want to hear how long they've been sober. Addicts count. I want to hear about the fruit of their sobriety, the death of passivity, financial turnarounds, reconciled relationships, greater intimacy with their wives, or fulfillment of a dream. Every three months or so just before testimony time I do a short teaching on this just as a reminder that we're looking to applaud the deeper outflow of the hard work, the suffering, the good choices. When we hear a good one, which is almost every time, we stand, we clap, and we celebrate it together.

If I know there is a good testimony in the room, I'll call that man up front without warning. These are the best as there is no time to prepare, so what he says is straight from the heart, just what we need. When someone really brings it raw and nails it we like to brag on them openly, highlighting what he did right and use it not just as an injection of hope, but as a teaching moment. Be careful not to upstage the guys giving testimonies, but show them the respect they deserve for a courageous act of honesty that sets other men free.

TALK

Talks should be short. If you are just getting started, talks should be very short, five minutes at most before you have small group. When you split to two groups, go with ten-minute talks and keep moving up the time as you grow. No matter how big you get, talks should never be more than thirty minutes. Men like speakers who say a lot in a short amount of time. Give it to them like a firehose, they'll love you for it.

The job of the speaker is to bring us face to face with God. Good speakers tell us the truth and are dangerously honest. Great speakers articulate our own thoughts and speak them back to us. They connect to us, and make us feel a part of something greater than ourselves. They show humility and speak with confidence. They are teachers and storytellers. They use metaphor and their own experience. Their lives may be messy, but they are getting better. They make us laugh. They often cry when they speak. They show us what is possible with God.

Our pulpit is a special place. Up front you're the best you there is. Brilliant things come out of my mouth that I have never thought about before up there. It's so good I'll go home and listen to the podcast and think, "Who is that guy?" You can't fake it up there. If you try, the men in the room can smell it. We have had several outside speakers who regularly speak to thousands of people come in and choke because the atmosphere of honesty is daunting. The men in the room are at a turning place in life. Many are hurting and being vulnerable for the first time, facing their hurt to heal.

They are very raw, they need the man on the pulpit to connect with them in that broken place. Be that man—not above them, but with them.

I was a communication major in college and focused on public speaking. I was good at it. When I came to Christ my junior year, I was undone. Within months I completely lost all ability from the podium. I became so insecure that it was difficult to speak to more than a few people. I have a long and painful story here, but the short of it is, it took me twenty years to dig myself out of that hole and be comfortable speaking publicly again. I didn't check out, I kept taking opportunities to speak when offered, but there were more losses than wins for a long time. God broke me down, and it took two decades to rebuild me in this area. I wouldn't want to do it again, but I'm glad it went the way it did. It's much less about the speaking than actually having something to say. Jonah had heat on what he had to say after being in the belly of the whale.[3] I wonder if Nineveh would have repented if he would have skipped the three-day belly of the whale ride. There has never been a good message that someone didn't suffer for. It's the price of great preaching.

Through the rebuilding process I learned a lot. Today one of my favorite, most satisfying things to do is to work with our speakers to make them better. I'm not running a charity. I put the best man in the room up to speak each week, but I work with him, a little before, and a little after. If I'm trying a new guy who has something to say, it's my job to help him get it out. I spend a lot more time with the new guys than with the more seasoned speakers.

Before you put a new guy up, let him open and close worship a few times. Let him lead the testimony time or give his own. Give him some exposure in the front so he feels the room and starts to build a connection.

I often pull up a guy I believe in and split a talk with him for his first time. If he screws it up, I can clean it up and it's all good. The best speaker we have ever had in the group fully messed up his

---

3. Jonah 1-3.

first talk. He was barely coherent. I put him up the next time in the summer on a holiday (I wasn't there because I take summers off) and I heard from everyone that he completely killed it. He was off and running after that. Failure is part of getting better. You don't want it to happen, but when it does, embrace it and learn.

When picking who will speak, you're the head chef and you want to serve a balanced meal. Create the best meal possible, and not just for taste or for the presentation. You want organic, nutrient-dense ingredients, high in protein, and raw. Look for guys who have the heat on them, those whom God is at work in their lives, guys that are yielding to him and getting results.

Never put up a speaker who has just lost job, or is temporarily unemployed. Never put up a speaker who has just gotten back from a trip, or right when they return from a break. Let them re-acclimate to the room, reconnect with the guys, and grab ahold of the vision again. Never put up a speaker on someone's recommendation. Go with who you want, who you're connected to. Go with your gut.

We have women speakers in about three times a year and once at Man-i-Fest because they have something we need. Men have a big woman deficit and having women in to speak touches that spot of feminine love, care, and comfort that we so desperately need. These women are our friends because they tell us the truth. They love us, and bring that mom atmosphere we desperately need. They carry with them comfort and care, honesty, and encouragement. Something happens inside each of us when they say, "I am proud of you guys, good job."

You need to have some level of relationship with every man or woman who takes your pulpit. If they're great, but you don't know them super well, spend some time with them just prior to speaking so you're connected. You'll never go wrong when you do this as they will have your heart for the men in the room.

Taylor showed up to group right out of high school, drowning in pornography. He ended up in a great group of older guys who were all struggling deeply with their own stuff. Seeing what decades of porn had done to the other men's lives, Taylor was impacted heavily and resolved to do whatever it took to get better. As he sobered up, he entered into a long season of pain. He would call guys all the time to get prayer, but when it was too late at night and no one would answer the phone, he would drive to the prayer house at church that is open 24/7 and cry his eyes out.

Taylor and his father, who is a pastor, had a very disconnected relationship. As Taylor got better, he wanted more in his relationship with his dad and told him everything. He poured out his heart starting with his sexual struggles. When he was done, his father was blown away, and in turn told him his own sexual struggles; the two have been very close ever since.

His dad was so moved by the event that he called and emailed me several times to thank me. He even loaded up some men from his church and made the long pilgrimage here, just to see what we were doing that had helped his son so much. Shortly after, those same men started a very successful sexual purity group in their church.

Taylor was in a long-term relationship with the love of his life. Together, they fully committed to purity and their relationship thrived. A year later they were married on the beach in a beautiful ceremony. I love to see them together as there is such a pure innocence about them and their friendship is strong.

I usually recommend (because of Deuteronomy 24:5) that newly married guys take a year off from group. Taylor would have none of it and didn't want to stop coming. He argued that what he did in group was a lifestyle that wouldn't change if he came to group or not. I gave in, and gave him a group to lead, which turned out to be excellent for everyone involved.

He has since moved twice in the last five years and has started a group in each place he has lived. Both have been very successful. A few months back I went to speak at his group and was blown away by the intimacy, the passion, and the fruit in the lives of the men in the room.

With his first child on the way, he is working, loving, and living life extraordinarily well, as well he should as there is so much more good to come.

It's very important to me that the man on the pulpit has a good marriage that is getting better. I want to know that he and his wife are aggressively working on their stuff, and that he is making decisions primarily with his family in mind. If you can see new life, hope, and excitement in the eyes of a man's wife, you know he's doing well. If a man is single, I look to see that he's determined to deal with his stuff—it's preparation for the family that is to come. To find the guys with the heat on them, I listen to what others are saying about them. I look for men who are leading by example and who are being followed by others, for men who may fail but are quick to humbly repent and get back at it. These are the men I want to hear speak.

I always call whoever is speaking a few days before to check in on them to make sure they're doing okay. I remind them that they have thirty minutes and not to go over. Often guys will have had a tough time in the days prior to a talk. So we work through it. I tell them it's very normal and since it's been hard, he'll now have heat on what he says because he's paid a price. I personally get a little worried if everything is perfect.

If it's a new speaker, I almost always hit them with this analogy: Speaking is like flying a plane. It's a lot of work to take it off and to land it, so spend your time on the take off and landing. Once you're up, fly straight to the landing and nail the landing, that's the most important part of the flight. You might not have a perfect handle on everything that comes out of your mouth and in what order, but know how you will begin and more importantly how you will end. Do this and you'll do well.

To me, a great speaker for what we're doing is based on how often he can bring a good word. You can find and work with great guys, but how often they can be great is the question. You have to find the line of frequency that is the right timeline for each man. The best speakers in the room are right at, or just under the two-month mark. Several are at the three-month mark, others are twice a year, and a handful only speak once in the summer. If you put a guy up too early, and if he hasn't fully processed what he needs to, what he says will come out choppy. If you wait too long, you miss the sweet spot and he is already on to the next thing and his message loses its heat because he is pulling it up from the past.

I don't control or direct the speakers. I try to help them pull out what is already there if they need it. When I give the pulpit away, it's the speaker's time and I trust him with it. I give a lot of encouragement, as speaking is a courageous act. If someone bombs (which doesn't happen very often) they know it, nothing much needs to be said. I just love them. It's easy for me since I have bombed more than anyone I know. Love and acceptance brings out the best in us all.

SMALL GROUP

The details of the small group are covered in the previous section, but there are a few more things that need to be addressed here regarding doing small group within the context of a larger men's group.

Be careful not to steal time from small group with longer segments of worship, testimonies, games, or talks. It is very important that we work extra hard to make sure small groups have a full hour. If you want to guarantee a bad night, just steal time from small group.

Some groups will meet before and eat together, other groups might go have a beer or a barbecue after the speaker is done. This is all great and encouraged; however, doing stuff together is not a replacement for doing small group. Respect the group time, that's where your men get better.

We don't try and figure out who goes in what group—it's just a God lottery. The first six guys to show up ready to start in a group are usually put into a group together. I like really diverse groups best, but the Holy Spirit brings who he brings when he brings them, so we roll with that.

If someone has a complaint about a group, I bring it back to the fact that God's leading is a factor in how groups are formed; that specific man came at the time he did in response to that leading to be with these specific men for their healing. Like them or not, those are the cards you were dealt, so play them. Many times it's the tough guys in the group that can bring the most healing. They push buttons in the other guys in the group that bring stuff up and make guys have to face it. It's uncomfortable and messy, but healing and beautiful.

No matter how big your group grows in numbers or how your responsibilities increase, let no one in the room ever be above leading or being in a small group. I lead a small group of new guys every year. Every time I sit down with a new group of guys, I'm never too excited about it, but two months later I'm in love with those men, happens every time.

SMALL GROUP LEADERS

What we are doing only works with great group leaders. The only things I promise our leaders are free food once month, that they will get better, and that by leading a group they will get better faster. It's a volunteer army, the pay is internal and eternal.

The best way to get good at leading is by watching and experiencing the leadership of someone who is good at doing it, and then doing it yourself. But here is a hot tip: Hang around after group and catch the men who are good at leading and ask them for help. Run situations by them and ask what they would do. There are great leaders in the room, make use of them.

Once a month we have a small group leader meeting and it always involves food. If you want the men to come, feed them. We get together an hour and a half before group and eat together. For fifteen minutes of that time I give a short talk. I start out by calling for testimonies about what is happening with their men, or with themselves. Always start with good news. Let it remind us all why we're doing what we're doing. We hear from other leaders. We get inspired about what God is doing among us. It's a faith builder.

Once we get a good fill of good news, I'll move down a list I bring of things to work on in your small group like active listening, homework, the importance of prayer, how to deal with tough guys, managing the clock, modeling, finding what brings us to life, and firmness and kindness and what that looks like. The list goes on and it's different every month according to the needs I see out there.

I always try to thank the leaders, and make it very clear how valuable they are, because group doesn't work without them. Often I'll have another group leader with a certain expertise do a short teaching about what they are doing in their small group, what works, what doesn't, and why.

We'll plan future events at these meetings, make short announcements, love each other, have a beer, slap high fives, laugh, do a lot of hugging, and have some beautifully intimate talks over some great food. One night it just came to me while I was speaking that we should take some time and pick out one man in the room and publicly thank him for what he means to us. When we were done, there was hardly a dry eye in the house. It made me wonder why we don't do that more often.

One of the best leader meetings that we ever had I passed out three by five cards to each man and asked them to write on the card the names of three men in the room they respect and a man they would call when they are in trouble or ask advice from. When they were done I said, "Look at your card, those men are your pastors." It was a beautiful moment, and very freeing for me. My phone used to ring multiple times a week, and since then it's only rung a few times a month. It's glorious. As a leader of this group, empowering the men to choose their own leaders was one of the smartest things I've ever done. From that moment on the room has been completely and naturally relational, just as it should be.

LARGE GROUP DYNAMICS

Plain and simple men, this is combat and passive men don't get free. Bringing down the things that hold us back is an act of violence.[4] Learn from those who have gone before us. Find the best and hang out with them. Get around them and let yourself be influenced. Read everything relevant you can get your hands on. Readers are leaders. Take comfort in the great and sometimes lesser-known military leaders of the past. You will be surprised at how similar the experience of combat is to running a group and will take courage from their words. Some of my favorites are George Patton, Ariel Sharon, Thomas Cochrane, Daniel Morgan, Lawrence of Arabia, Napoleon, Horatio Nelson, Gangus Khan, and David.

One thing to add here is that it is very important to have a peer in the room when you're leading the large group, someone who knows you and complements what you're doing. This person needs to have enough relational change with you to be able to point out problems or weak spots. Hold the vision, but listen to everything he says, because he has insight that you don't.

When the group really starts to grow and the intimacy is deep, the worship is moving, the honesty is uncomfortably beautiful and freeing, this is when you really start having church. Your group can and will start to feel more like the church than the church. At this point, make sure you don't reject the church in any way. It's very important that we never become an Absalom or raise a hand against the Lord's anointed.[5] You might be in a bad place and catch the king taking a crap, cut off a piece of his robe, and wave it around, but you'll get convicted for it. After twenty plus years of Jesus freaking, I have recognized that it doesn't go well for men who reject the church. So when the chips are down, no matter how bad it hurts, never reject the church. Repeat after me, never reject the church.

4. 2 Corinthians 10:4.
5. 2 Samuel 16–18, 1 Samuel 24.

> Just before Jason started coming to group he decided to tell his wife about his pornography problem. She said, "It feels like you are cheating on me, but I know that you aren't. I will do whatever it takes to help you get better." The way she handled it was a huge part of him getting better as fast as he did.
>
> After just a few weeks in group, he started crying and didn't stop for over a year. Every time I saw him he was crying. Crying in group, crying while giving a testimony, crying when I would talk to him. His tears were not sad, they were tears of relief. They were cleansing, tears of happiness. I asked him once why he was crying all the time. He said, "Because of the difference between what I had believed about myself and what God really thinks about me."
>
> He attends another church in town and is on the worship team. With a new set of tools and with a confident honesty guiding him, he started making a huge impact on his home church to such an extent that the pastor has him speak several times a year at multiple services.
>
> There are a lot of great stories here but only so much space, but know that he was a key player in a revival among the youth in his church as well. Great stuff. He is a hard worker and doing better and better at work and going after his passions.
>
> He struggled initially with the fear of becoming a father because of father issues. But much of that was healed by continual touches of the Holy Spirit and his constant pursuit of healthy men in the room that helped him along the way. He asked for help, and he got it. Men love him and today he is a father in the natural and in the room and doing great at both.

There will sometimes be church politics, misunderstandings, and pastoral concerns. It's just life in the trenches. Adjust your methods if needed, and work on your word choices, but don't water things down. If there is a problem, make sure that you're not it. Leading and running a group is difficult, but never boring. It's a challenge that is worth the effort. Be patient. Time and the fruit of changed lives makes everything come out in the wash.

ATMOSPHERE

It's not your job get men better; it's your job to create an atmosphere for them to get better in. The difference between doing those two things is the same as the difference between digging a ditch in rocky ground and lying at the beach. The very best thing you can do for the men is be yourself and never do anything out of obligation unless it's to feed your family. Be the full masculine you without apology. Do what you do because you want to, because you love it. When you do that, it's contagious. Equip, connect, and empower and let them do the rest.

When we break to go to group we play three songs to nurture the atmosphere we've created while we transition.[6] We also have videos going with no volume on two screens at the same time as the music is playing. The videos are of bull riding, motorcycle racing, mountain climbing, football, UFC, and hockey highlights. People Are Awesome videos are great too. Let these run for about ten minutes while guys mill around, talk, hug, and go to their groups. We just spent an hour setting them up for small group with worship, testimonies, games, and the talk. The music and videos of men doing what makes them come alive is the dessert to an excellent meal.

LEADERSHIP STRUCTURE

Leadership in the room should be natural. The leaders are who the leaders are—they don't need titles. Leadership teams get in the way of relationship. We're the Knights of the Round Table, everyone has equal input. The weight of a leader's influence is equal to the

---

6. For example, here are a few of my favorites: "H.O.L.Y." by Florida Georgia Line; "I Wanna Get Better" by Bleachers; "My Church" by Maren Morris; "Humble and Kind" and "Live Like You Were Dying" by Tim McGraw; "A Heart Like Mine" by Miranda Lambert; "Should Have Been a Cowboy" by Toby Keith; "God Gave Me You" by Blake Shelton; "Boondocks" by Little Big Town; "I Wont Back Down" by Tom Petty; "Sweetly Broken" by Jeremy Riddle; "Beer with Jesus" by Thomas Rhett; "God Bless the Broken Road" by Rascal Flats. And the list goes on.

fruit of his life and his commitment to the overall betterment of the men in the room.

I liken our leadership in the room to what David did outside the walls of Jerusalem before the Israelites captured it and made it their home. He looked around and said, "Who wants to be in charge? Whoever goes in there and kills the most Jebusites is the leader." A Jebusite represents sexual sin as it holds the very place in which we were meant to worship. Joab was the first in and received the command. Then David rebuilt the city, which became the central place of worship for all Israel.[7] Our leaders are those who do the same. They take ground, create a place to worship, and rebuild.

Men who need help should reach out on their own initiative and pull on other men whom they respect. They do this by asking questions while finding a way to help their leader (wash his car, change out a battery, etc.), listening to his answers, then doing what he says. If you're going to ask your leader for advice and you get some, make a smart move and do what he says, even if you don't understand it, he does. A Jebusite-killer has been there before, he knows what to do. Listen and act. The student should pursue the mentor, not the other way around.

For what we do and the way we do it, I like a strong central leader. This is the guy who runs the group and has no problem giving it up if someone, over time, is more qualified than he is. He holds on lightly, yet is deeply committed to the men. He listens to everyone, and can quickly implement changes when needed without a committee. He is ever-learning through the lives of others and growing in his relationship with God. He is there to heal himself; he hasn't arrived. He is humble yet confident in the call on his life. He makes the final and prayerfully weighed decisions, and lives with the fallout. He loves the men, and they love him back. He honors the church and lives gracefully. He protects the confidentiality of the men in the room. He gives strength and imparts hope to those who fail. He can acknowledge it when he himself fails. He loves Jesus, his family, and

---

7. 1 Chronicles 11:4–9.

his church. He is a good provider. He is on a mission to get better and take as many men with him as possible.

Naaman, a great man and commander of an army, had leprosy and came to Elisha to be healed.[8] He showed up with his entourage. Elisha told him to go take a dip in the sewer and he would be healed. He got mad, but was smart enough to listen to the friend who talked him into taking the swim. It was an act of humility that got him healed. Likewise men, we have to swallow our pride and get down in the sewer to get clean.

BREAKING VOWS, RENOUNCING BELIEFS, NAMING DREAMS

This is important to do once a year in group. First teach on it and give an example of how it's done. Then let the men work on their vows and beliefs for a week and come back and do it as a group in place of the talk the following week.

A vow is a decision we make in reaction to being hurt. For instance, if you had a terrible public speaking experience, you might decide that you will never speak again. Or if your father hurt you really badly, you might make a vow that you will never be like your father. If one of your plans failed in a big way, you can create a belief that you are a failure, that nothing you ever do works out, that you don't have what it takes.

Breaking vows needs to happen because those vows keep us out of relationship. We need relationships. They may have hurt us, but it's relationships that will heal us. Beliefs become lies that we begin to live out of. What is not true has to go.

Breaking vows publicly is extremely powerful. Every year we do it and every time there are lots of tears as men let go of what has been holding up their healing. Breaking vows is my favorite night of the year. There are all these fantastic insights that come out. I find myself in the words of many of the men. I feel their pain. I experience their new-found freedom. I hear their dreams.

---

8. 2 Kings 5.

Josh's Story: At thirty-seven years old I did not have hope to live a life free from watching porn and masturbating on a regular basis. I had sworn I would quit so many times I lost count. I had no restraint in my life. I would even watch porn on my phone while driving to and from my home. I had no self-control when gone for business to a hotel and pretty much any time I was home alone. As each year of failure passed, I further cemented my belief in the lie that it was not possible to live in freedom. I lied to myself, my friends, family, church, and my wife every time she asked if I was struggling.

My self-medication was in the way of me pushing myself to do difficult things, took away all genuine intimacy with my precious wife, and stunted my growth with Jesus to the point where I was doubting his existence. I had "accountability" partners in the past and as soon as I would lie to them once, I could do it every time.

I had constant anger to the point of storming out of the house, driving unsafely, and punching holes in the walls of my home. I looked good on the outside but was dead on the inside—rotting spiritually, emotionally, and relationally. I didn't want to pursue God, lead my family, or use my free time wisely. I was acting out in secret, and it was playing out negatively in every area of my life. I was so selfish I almost missed out on adopting my precious daughter because I didn't want to put myself in an uncomfortable place. She has since changed my life forever for the better.

I was caught in yet another lie when I decided to let the chips fall where they would and came clean to my wife. This led to a devastation that looked impossible to recover from. I had burned her too many times throughout our marriage of seventeen years and I thought it might end. Her pain and immediate loss of trust was extremely difficult to endure. There were tears, screaming, anger, and desperation that didn't last just hours, day, or months. It lasted over a year and still can be triggered.

When I confessed to my wife, I went straight to sobriety as a promise to try to retain her. I saw it as my last "do-over" before I just gave up forever.

She asked that I attend a group that was led by the husband of one of her friends. I was very afraid to walk through the doors. However, after listening to Mark speak at ManAlive and feeling offended, desperate, and hopeful all at the same time, I couldn't get there fast enough to sign up for a group.

Group taught me I was not alone, how to talk, and to tell the whole

> truth (which led to more pain for both my wife and myself, but was absolutely necessary).
>
> I am now nearly two years sober, which I had believed was absolutely impossible, and the life that I have now is unrecognizable from before. The intimacy between my wife and I is complete. We talk about absolutely everything and broken connection is rare.
>
> Her trust is building and she celebrates sobriety with me each month. I work hard to maintain her trust and will share with her how I'm doing without her needing to ask. I err on the side of sharing too much. This has created confidence in her with me and further intimacy and deep communication. Our sex life is to be envied. I had no idea it was possible to love someone this deeply and selflessly. I have no fear to talk to my kids about anything. I have become bold and more successful in business and am becoming less passive with each interaction that I have the opportunity to act in. I can't wait each week to be with the men that breathe life into me at men's group, and I am blown away when my life story helps change another man's life because of what has changed in me the last two years.
>
> More importantly than anything else, I have completely surrendered to Jesus, and I now live my life on my knees before him. I have no desire to move from that place. Life is sweet where I am. I love it, and feel redeemed.

It's beautiful.

When you do it, limit the number of vows men can read so it doesn't go on forever and you can get to small group on time. Ten is a good number. Each man should stand up front and say their vows like this (I'll use the examples I gave above.):

I renounce the vow that I will never speak publicly again.
I renounce the vow that I will never be like my father.
I renounce the belief that I am a failure.
I renounce the lie that says I don't have what it takes.

We do one clap corporately after each vow and belief is broken. It feels good as it's a physical sign of a spiritual event. Breaking vows, killing bad beliefs, and naming our dreams instantly deepens the intimacy of the room. When we're seen at the origin of our pain we are known like never before. It breaks off the normal and allows us to be seen corporately. It's an isolation killer that allows us to feel loved, not by just one, but by many. It's a game changer.

On dreams, allow one maybe two dreams one sentence long that they add at the end of their list of vows and false beliefs. They should not be things like I want to marry the woman of my dreams, be a good father, husband, or I want to own my own business, because those are all things that are going to happen as you get better. That's a natural outflow of a man coming alive, living holy, getting better. We're looking for dreams like: I'm going to swim the Strait of Gibraltar, run with the bulls, hike the entire Pacific Crest Trail, race the Baja 1000, be the first one to ride a horse around the world, grow all my own food, live in a cave in Tibet for a year. We're not looking for spiritual dreams either. We want to know the man and what he wants for himself. The family, business, all the God stuff, it's going to happen. With dreams, for our purposes, we're looking for the masculine, the raw, the real, or the unique.

When you do this right, it teaches men to recognize when they have been hurt, when they make a vow, when they embrace a wrong belief, and to take care of it on the spot so they don't have to carry it for years. The tears you will see when you do this is from men who have done just that. Breaking vows frees them from the past and preempts the carrying of unnecessary pain. When you mix the dreams in at the end, it's a cool combination of letting go of the hurt along with the hope of what is to come.

MONEY

The reward in leading a group is eternal treasure. It's satisfying to play a role in changing the direction of a man's life. I regularly get emails, texts, and calls from men, (locally, from around the country, and now internationally) thanking me for building a place where they could get better. The overwhelming theme is: "Thank you, you saved my life." Treasure in heaven is a great reward but the light bill needs to be paid too. Here's our story, yours will be different because of the church you're in and the way you do things.

We ran the group for almost three years and got up to around seventy-five men with nothing more than an occasional donation. I was very clear when we started, and still am today, that we do this group in the church. That means we run our money through the church, we meet in the church, and have no intention of becoming a parachurch organization.

Today, we charge a one-time fee of 200 dollars, and ask for a six-month commitment. I wrestled with charging a fee for a long time and expected provision from other places, but it was pretty lean. I talked to my pastoral oversight at the time, and they both said I should start charging. One suggested a small amount a week. I went with a variation of that with the one-time fee, and it's worked really well for us. I was really uncomfortable charging for about six months, and then the light went on and we haven't looked back.

When men have to pay up to fix a problem they can't manage on their own, it's a humbling experience. That humility and desperation gets them where they need to be to start the process of getting better. When a guy turns in the paperwork and his check, he has skin in the game. He's not just checking it out anymore, he's going for it. The fee really helps with the commitment level, and it helps us pay the bills, so it's good both ways. I would recommend that you run your group at no cost until you build some good momentum. At least a year, two may be better. We started charging about three years into it. In retrospect, right at two years in would have been best.

We spend our money on food for the small group leader feeds that we have once a month just before group. The games often need materials, and we always give away a prize. Also, all outside speakers get paid. Some have refused to take money, which is very cool, so we'll slip them a gift card to their favorite restaurant or something that fits them, just to show some love for them for coming in. Of the hundreds of men in the room, two are on staff at church and get paid a portion of their salary for helping with group. Other than myself, it's all volunteers, men who want to be there wholeheartedly.

Getting paid to run the group never crossed my mind in the early years. I certainly didn't start it with that in mind. Into the fourth year, because of our growth, there started being a surplus. So I was able to receive a small amount each month, as I have kids to feed too. I am self-employed and have been the vast majority of my life, so it was weird at first, but then later it became nice to receive. More than anything for me, it's nice to be valued.

Later that year my pastoral oversight arranged that our church would start to help monthly as well and added some acorns to the tree, so that was really nice. Shortly after that, donations started to come in on a more regular basis. I thank those who give one time sincerely and say something along the lines of, "Thank you for that gift, may it return to you many times." And it will. We're good ground, one hundred fold ground, the kind of soil you're looking to plant in.

So here we are, running a successful and mostly self-sustaining group that feels great to go to each week. It takes time to get there, but we're changing lives and creating and sustaining both personal and corporate revival, while blessing the families within our church at the same time. It's a good deal.

An excellent financially freeing suggestion is to take an offering a few times a year. It's good for men to give. We find a worthy cause that is relationally connected, tell the story, and pass the hat. I am regularly surprised at the generosity. It's fun to give it away. It's one of my favorite things to do. Giving is an act that helps break the selfish addictive mind-set.

MOVING ON, OR NOT

The cool part about the group—why I keep coming and why men who get what is going on rarely leave—is that we keep getting better together. What we do in the room becomes a lifestyle; it's not just a check-this-off-the-list fulfillment of a program. The deeper we dig, the better relationships we have and the more alive we become. There are levels to our sexual freedom. It starts with getting sober and keeps going deeper and deeper and it spreads from there to improve the other areas where we struggle. Through it we get to know and love ourselves more and more over time. Each deeper place you go makes you feel lighter, happier, and stronger. We're going after radical self-improvement and it's working. That's why we keep doing it because we just keep getting better.

I don't ever pressure anyone to stay. Leave freely when you want to. This is a voluntary army. A bunch of guys move every year when school is over, so we expect that. On average we lose one leader a year who is just done coming, and I'm good with that if they are in a good place. Most are so hooked by the process and intimacy we have in the room and can't find a replacement for it elsewhere, so they stay. Plus, as you're getting better, so are the men you are leading in your small group. It's really rewarding to see their lives change, their marriages get better, prosperity at work in their lives, and the healing and reestablishing of their relationships. The pay is good because it's eternal.

There is a lot of talk and statistics about abortion, child pornography, and sex slavery, and a lot of great people doing some pretty positive things to combat these problems, as well they should. But with that said, the things on that list are all symptoms of the problem. When the demand is gone, the supply will be gone as well. By continuing to push in and pursue purity we change ourselves and the atmosphere around us. By changing us, we change the world.

MAN-I-FEST

Man-i-Fest is a weekend when our group as a whole goes up to Need Camp at Whiskeytown Lake. We eat some great food, breathe some mountain air, and get plenty dirty. Guys look forward to it all year. A big hit was the Highland Games. We painted our faces blue, threw spears, flipped logs, heaved boulders, and carried weights for long distances. We had a giant slip and slide, a manually operated bull to ride, and a huge relay race that featured some of the best games of the year at once. This year we're doing a western theme. It will be one for the record books for sure.

It's good to get out of town and be together. We've built some great traditions that we all look forward to each year. We give out awards for most improved, most honest man in the room, and there is an ongoing wide array of games and contests that will get and keep your blood pumping. It's pretty cool after eating a pound-of-meat-per-person barbecue (brought to us by the Odell brothers) to have a bunch of men worshiping together around a big bonfire with an ice-cold river running fifty feet away in the background. It's just good for the heart, it re-centers you, and you come down from the mountain knowing the guys in your small group in a whole new way.

We have men leaving Redding every year and starting groups all over the country, and now a handful internationally. All those men in a group are invited back to Man-i-Fest each year, and it's like a big family reunion. It's good for the soul to hear the testimonies and to catch up. The cool part about seeing old friends that fully commit to going after God wholeheartedly is that it's like no time has passed, and you can pick up right where you left off.

If you have a group in your home church that follows the principles of ManAlive then you are invited to come. Traditionally we have it the first weekend of May, watch for the dates and info at imanalive.com.

YOU TOO

A few years back a few friends and I went to a U2 concert in Oakland. Our seats were on the lower part of the upper level and once we found them, two guys sat down, and I went with another friend to grab some drinks. On the way back, coming out of the tunnel to get into the arena, I was moved by the sea of people and the energy in the air. It was the time in between the warm-up band and U2 coming out on stage. In the moment, I saw my two friends at our seats and raised my arms and shouted, "HEY!!!" I was surprised to see about ten other people in our section stand up with their arms in the air and yell, "HEY!" right back at me.

Without thinking I yelled, "Let's start a wave!" I counted off and got about 100 people going. The next time, we were up to about 1,000. Now starting to lose my courage, I thought to myself, "I'll give it one more try." This time we got the whole upper level going (probably more than 10,000 people), but the wave didn't pass the break in the stadium to make it fully around.

I was thinking, "Well that's it. Nice try," when somebody, way up in the back, yelled, "DON'T GIVE UP, YOU CAN DO IT!" With my courage renewed, I went for it one more time with a new passion. I even ran with the wave for a long time after starting it. The wave made it past the stadium break this time and all the way around. It increased in intensity and then started on the next level down, then the next level down started too. We were doing it together, but each level was at a different speed, going round and round, louder and louder. It was beautiful, and I had a moment.

People were coming from all over our section to pat me on the back and say, "Good job. Way to go! We knew you could do it." The wave went on longer than any I have ever seen, it just kept going and going, and it didn't stop until Bono stepped onto the stage. People were having fun, and I was a proud father.

***

The dream, gentlemen, is a ManAlive group in every church on the globe. A place where men find a home and a family inside their church. Great victories are won when one man like Shammah gets tired of running and defends a field of beans.[9] He didn't have much, but he defended what he had, turning the tide of the battle

---

9. 2 Samuel 23:11.

and bringing about a great victory.

It's time for a group in your church and you're the man for the job. Your church and the men in it need one man to defend a field of beans and turn the tide. They need one man to stand up and yell, "HEY!!!" And another, at just the right time, to say, "DON'T GIVE UP, YOU CAN DO IT."

FIVE SMOOTH STONES

I WROTE MANALIVE TO BE AS SHORT AND POIGNANT AS POSSIBLE so that men who don't read much might take a shot at it because of its brevity. Below are five must read blog posts I wrote on imanalive.com. They cover subjects that didn't make the book and need to be read. Like the five smooth stones of David, they're giant killers.

GO TO WWW.IMANALIVE.COM AND SEARCH THESE TITLES:
1. CHAINSAW
2. MASTURBATION, THE GOOD NEWS
3. THE ULTIMATE MAN MODEL
4. NO PLACE YOU WOULD RATHER BE
5. HOLIDAY SEX

Made in the USA
San Bernardino, CA
27 January 2018